Savage Sales Secrets

Downers Grove Public Library
1050 Curtiss St.
Downers Grove, IL 60515
(630) 960-1200
www.downersgrovelibrary.org

What others say about Steve's Savage Sales Secrets

Steve Savage is the **greatest guerrilla experimenter** I know and is willing to take the risks that must be faced high on the ladder to the top.

> Jay Levinson, Author
> Guerrilla Marketing. USA

I have never seen anyone who could organize a business, recruit a sales force and motivate the entire company, better than Steve Savage. He is a **genuine business visionary**.

> Rod Turner, Senior Executive Vice President
> Colgate Palmolive. USA

Steve's **ideas flow from a lifetime of real experiences** of running his own companies throughout the Western Hemisphere.

> Victor Post, Director for Latin America
> Kohler Corporation, USA

Steve's ideas are practical and achievable. He recognizes that 80% of strategy is implementation and therefore doesn't stop until his strategies are actionable, **changing corporate culture** to make a business totally customer-friendly.

> Harry Strachan
> Director Emeritus, Bain and Company, USA and Costa Rica

Microsoft strives to help our customers find easier, more effective and innovative ways to achieve their goals. Steve Savage's ideas and experiences are "**straight, down-to-earth recipes**."

> René Picado, Regional Director
> Microsoft Central America

Steve's sales and marketing seminars were well received in Costa Rica, El Salvador, Guatemala, Panama, Nicaragua and Honduras. They served to **open the eyes of many** in terms of opportunities in those markets.

> Carlos Denton, General Manager
> Gallup Central America

Baba Steve! We are smiling for the joy you bring to us when we think of you. Thank you BABA for being a pillar of strength. Thanks for your **words of wisdom and motivation**. You are God sent. Steve, you are **our mentor and the big brain behind our business**. You know what? You ROCK!!!

> Phindile Sithole and Bomkazi Bhengu, Partners
> Soul of South Africa Enterprises

Steve did an outstanding job, building the business from zero to $15,000,000 in 4 years. He has high energy level, sense of vision, relentless creativity, marketing and sales ability, people skills and a **unique ability to articulate his thoughts and experiences**.

> E. Peter Raisbeck, Chairman
> Institutional Financing Services, USA

After three years of flat sales, in June we started Steve Savage's new sales strategy. **Our sales grew 18% in July, 31% in August and 56% in September**. He not only gave us recommendations, but he implemented his plan.

> Mario Simán, President
> Unicomer. El Salvador

Steve Savage transformed our Eastern Region, which had flat sales for several years, into a fast-growing network of warehouses. He organized a nationwide telemarketing operation and **gained 3,471 new customers in 12 months**.

> Mike Rippey, President
> Radiator Express Warehouse, USA

It's true Steve Savage style...**punchy, articulate, compelling and value added for the reader**. Very nice job!

> Jim Cascino, CEO
> Discovery Toys, USA

You certainly have some **incredible experiences**. It was great to have you put it all into a single, coherent series of stories that makes sense.

> Jeff Titterington, President
> AEON Capital Consultants, USA

I love your book! Truly, it's eminently readable and filled with interesting and helpful information. I like that you **convey your "secrets" via stories** since we are much more likely to remember stories than facts and figures.

> Pamela Enders, Ph.D.
> Winner's Circle Coaching, USA

Wow! What a great book! Your book is extremely strong and provides **really high-value**. A great achievement. It is an accurate projection of your many years of hands-on experience and mentoring skills.

> Roger Parker
> Author of 38 books including *Get Clients Now!* USA

Steve Savage worked with our sales force, going out to visit our clients in various provinces throughout Panama. Then he helped us with our sales and marketing strategy. He motivated us and **our sales increased 9%**.

> Dr. Dagoberto Tuñón, Marketing Director
> MELO Industries, Panama

You have touched and helped many people. Sure, "selling" is the purpose of what you promote, but the real magic of your interaction with people and what you promote is the effect it has on **helping people find the courage, self-confidence and fun in their lives** through career/work/economic activity.

> Fred Denton, General Manager
> La República Newspaper, Costa Rica

I have always said that **you are a GENIUS** – I learned more from you than I have learned in 26 years of reading business books. Thanks, Steve, for being a great SALES LEADER

Steve Conger, Regional Manager
Cherrydale Fundraising, USA

I absolutely love the book! I read it on the treadmill and I create quite a scene when I break out **laughing at all the sales incidents**!!! All those other people don't know what they missed in life by not being a salesperson!

Joe Arciniega, Vice President
America's Lemonade Stand, USA

We are an accounting firm. Steve came and showed us how to treat our customers with kindness and enthusiasm. We now have loyal **customers who will not go anywhere else** for their accounting business!

Gabriel Estevez, Partner
Estevez, Alvarez & Associates, Mexico

Thank you for the **magnificent knowledge which you provided for us**. It is not every day we get people in Angola of the quality of knowledge of Steve Savage. You were very good and immensely useful.

Tatiana Mourinha, Marketing Director
Unitel, Angola

Steve helped me found a new business. He helped me **get rid of my "corporate mentality" and adapt the "savage" mentality** which helped me succeed as a small business. We were very successful and we continue to grow.

Igor Zambrano, President
Sales Solutions, Venezuela

Steve Savage helped us set up a new business, training our salespeople, visiting our customers and **forming our business strategy**. We grew to $2,000,000 (USA) in our first two years.

Arturo Hotton, President
IFS de Argentina

Steve's teaching and enthusiasm have been the **determining factor in the growth of our company**. He has the added benefit of his perfect command of the Spanish language.

> Tomás Fortson, General Director
> Beneficio Escolar, Mexico

Steve changed the way we do business. I realized it was not enough to be just a "little bit better" but dramatically better. He taught me to go out in the field with my salespeople. He taught me to **treat my salespeople as heroes.**

> Salvador Parras, President
> Trolex, Mexico

Most consultants merely consult. Steve goes way beyond consulting and **gets things done**.

> Dennis Snyder, Chairman
> Meland Outreach, USA

All our executives now go out and visit customers, like Steve Savage recommended. It has **changed the culture of our company and increased sales**.

> Jorge González, General Manager
> Latin American Financial Services, Nicaragua

I started feeling energetic and began to change the way we do business. I am an introvert, but **you gave me the confidence that I could lead my sales and marketing team**. Thank you for your guidance and moral support.

> Akbar Umatiya, General Manager
> ATG, United Arab Emirates

Steve gave us direction on our telemarketing efforts. We launched a telephone drive and **gained 34,150 clients in three months**.

> Albaluz Soriano, Marketing Manager
> Telecom, El Salvador

Thank you for your participation in our program. **You provided new and beneficial information to all our members**. I have enjoyed working with you over this past year.

> Allison L. Manny, Director of Development and Education
> New York State Association of Health Care Providers, USA

Every manager developed a greater sense of responsibility to their respective organizations and their staff members. You delivered a **message of organizational culture in the office that truly provoked thought and opened minds**.

> DeeDee McIntyre, Assistant Vice President
> Heritage Bank, USA

Thank you for your brilliant participation in our annual convention of the Mexican Association of Direct Sales. You created a positive atmosphere with great audience involvement. All **our CEO's, who are experts in sales, learned new ideas from you** that will benefit each of them.

> Cecilia Carranza, General Manager
> Mexican Association of Direct Sales, Mexico

Savage Sales Secrets

29 Proven Strategies for Profitable Sales

By

STEVE SAVAGE

New York

Savage Sales Secrets
29 Proven Strategies for Profitable Sales
Copyright © 2010 Stephen E. Savage. All rights reserved.

Cover Design by: Rachel Lopez Rachel@r2cdesign.com

ISBN: 978-1-60037-690-0 (Paperback)

Library of Congress Control Number: 2009933974

MORGAN · JAMES
THE ENTREPRENEURIAL PUBLISHER

Morgan James Publishing, LLC
1225 Franklin Ave., STE 325
Garden City, NY 11530-1693
Toll Free 800-485-4943
www.MorganJamesPublishing.com

In an effort to support local communities, raise awareness and funds, Morgan James Publishing donates one percent of all book sales for the life of each book to Habitat for Humanity. Get involved today, visit **www.HelpHabitatForHumanity.org.**

Dedication

To Barrie, my wife, who voluntarily chose to become a "Savage" and has been my business partner as well as the love of my life for 38 years. She is my true *Savage Sales Secret*—and the only one I won't share with you!

Acknowledgements

Ted Welch opens this book as he opened my life to sales when I was a 19-year-old college student. Spencer Hays taught me how to make a salesperson feel incredibly important. Henry Bedford opened doors for me to interview many key people who contributed their *sales secrets* to this book.

Jay Levinson taught me how to write a powerful sales letter. He showed me how to open closed doors through authoritative direct mail and irresistible incentives. David Hancock enthusiastically promoted my previous book, **Guerrilla Business Secrets**, and wholeheartedly encouraged me to dig deeply and expand universally with **Savage Sales Secrets**.

Cheryl McElhose was the first woman salesperson in an all-guys' sales force. It was my honor to be her sales manager. Martha Serrano led the way for women in our Mexican sales force. Gloria Bauder in Venezuela proved that a 40-year-old divorced mother with four children could outsell all the men.

Harry Strachan opened up the world of consulting for me and introduced me to numerous clients. Carlos and Fred Denton made me well-known throughout Central America. Alan Weiss encouraged me to establish my own *Savage* brand. Chad Barr revolutionized my web site. Mike Rippey and Dennis Snyder have been my partners, friends and inspiration since 1968.

Dustin and Kyah Hillis are champions because they have no mental limits. Gary Michels built a great company through basic no-nonsense salesmanship. Rory Vaden got me to "take the stairs" instead of the elevator. Dave Brown dazzled me with his ability to meet thirty people and remember all their names. Amanda Johns knows everything you need to know about selling to the opposite gender. Tom Belli has prospered through brilliant product development, incredible service and creative sales leadership.

Carl Roberts built the perfect example of an ideal "intrapreneurial" company. Jeff Dobyns proved you can sell stocks and mutual funds without high pressure.

Jim Savage, my brother, and Pat Fuller showed me how health insurance should be sold. Cynthia Savage, my daughter, and Nick Yates showed me how health food products should be sold. Matt Savage, my son, showed me how appraisal services should be sold to mortgage companies and banks.

Steve Krochmal and Herb Kristal taught me that meticulous preparation results in an almost automatic close. Mimi Graves proved that knowing your client and your product leads to a sale based on a perfect match of the two.

Tomás Fortson has courage, guts and determination in overcoming incredible odds to survive and thrive.

Contents

Introduction

By Jay Conrad Levinson

As all guerrilla marketers know, people react more warmly and surely when you tell a story than when you relate a fact. Steve Savage's superb book of secrets is superb not only for the secrets themselves, but also because of the true-life, honest-to-goodness stories that breathe life into many of them.

You cannot help but sense that as you read this unique book, learning key facts that can revolutionize your business and your profits, but knowing that you'll remember what you're reading for a long time because it is far more memorable than a dry fact.

I've known Steve long enough and closely enough to also know that you're holding a precious key in your hands—a key that will solve problems before they arise and help you sidestep pitfalls with foresight and wisdom. The key I'm talking about is the power and majesty of knowledge, especially that knowledge which is lacking in the minds of your competitors. Some of that knowledge is so undiscovered that it is still a secret. The cream of those secrets have found their way into these pages as Steve stumbled upon them or learned them by dint of experience and pain balanced by rapture, the rapture of getting it right and knowing you can keep it right.

The thing I most remember about Steve is his ability to make clear that which is dense and confusing. He has always been able to use five words where most people use ten or twenty. He has x-ray vision for the heart of the matter. And he smiles a lot, all real smiles that you'll feel in his stories.

Those smiles come from his heart. I congratulate you on the smiles that will come from yours as you learn these 29 secrets and put them to work in your business and your life.

Foreword

Savage. What a name! Imagine being a kid in the sixth grade with the last name *Savage*. Kids used to make fun of me. I was embarrassed. I hated my name.

Fast forward. My speaking coach, the famous and marvelous Patricia Fripp, is pushing me ahead, telling me how to maximize my talents, how to create and promote my brand. "Steve!" she declared. "Your name! *Savage*! What a superb name. Promote it. Use it. Embellish it. Dramatize it. Brand it."

Thank you, my dear Patricia.

Yes, *Savage* is a great name and I thank my ancestors, from the ancient "*Sauvages*" (men of the woods in France), to the 31 Savages who were involved in America's Revolutionary War, to my unforgettable grandfather, Henry Savage, and my magnificent father, Robert Savage.

"*Savage,*" according to Webster's, means:

1. Fierce, ferocious, or cruel; untamed: savage beasts.
2. Uncivilized; barbarous: savage tribes.
3. Enraged or furiously angry, as a person.
4. Unpolished; rude: savage manners.
5. Wild or rugged, as country or scenery: savage wilderness.
6. Archaic. Uncultivated; growing wild.
7. An uncivilized human being.
8. A fierce, brutal, or cruel person.

For **Savage Sales Secrets**, let's choose a few of the above definitions: *wild, rugged, fierce and untamed.* These are words and principles that will guide our discussions throughout this book.

We will be *contrarian, different and unconventional.* But the ideas you will get in this book *work.* They have been proven by me and by several companies I have founded and built. They have also been proven by dozens of companies that I have guided as a consultant. They have been proven by brilliant sales leaders I have interviewed and whose ideas and techniques I share with you. Apply them and I guarantee you will succeed.

Savage Sales Secret #1

Get high production without high pressure

Yes! You can do it. You can *produce without pressure*. You can *close a sale without pressure*.

How? Let me tell you how I first began to learn my "***Savage Sales Secrets***."

My sales manager was *Ted Welch*. He opened up a fascinating new world for me when I was a sophomore in college. I worked my way through college selling books door-to-door. Ted was low-keyed with me as a manager. He got me to *produce without pressuring me*. He showed me how to *sell a huge volume without pressuring my customers*.

The Southwestern Company of Nashville, Tennessee helps college students manage their own sales business during their summer break. We attended a five-day sales school in Nashville. We then relocated to another community in another state, to foster independence and limit distractions. My first summer was in Columbus, Mississippi. My family was from Michigan. This was my first adventure in the Deep South. It was the greatest adventure of my young life.

After two days of knocking on doors by myself, Ted came to see me. That is when I learned my first ***Savage Sales Secrets*** principle.

> - You, the sales manager, must *get in the trenches* and visit your customers with your sales people.
> - A *Savage Sales Manager* does not sit in the office all the time.
> - He or she gets out—often—and gets on the front lines with the troops.

There is nothing harder than door-to-door sales, but Ted made it fun. He also made it profitable. I spent five summers selling books and six summers in college, until I got my MBA at Michigan State University. I learned more in those five summers of selling than I did in six years of college. I also graduated with money in the bank, stocks and a car, whereas most of my classmates were deeply in debt.

A soft approach

Ted taught me a "soft" approach to a customer. We would always ask who lived next door, so we had a name. We also found out where the kids went to school. (We were selling Webster's Dictionary and Student Handbook.) So the approach went like this: "Hi, Mrs. Jones. I'm Steve Savage. I'm calling on the folks whose kids go to Washington Elementary. Do you have a place we could sit down?" (Ted taught me to *talk very slowly*, which was definitely not my normal speed!)

About half the time we sat down. If not, we just chatted standing up. In either case, we were relaxed.

A soft presentation

Ted also taught me how to make a "soft" presentation. The best way to do that is to *ask a lot of questions*. That way the customer is engaged. "What grade is Johnny in? What is his best subject? What is his toughest subject? Who is Johnny's favorite teacher? Do you know Mrs. Smith next door? She liked this section because she thought it would help Susie with her math."

> - Ted felt that the salesperson should do only 50% of the talking.
> - Let the customer do the other 50%.

A soft close

When we came to the close, we always gave the customer a choice between "yes" and "yes." "If it would be *more convenient*, you can pay for these books today and I'll leave them with you right now. If it would *be easier*, you can wait and I'll deliver them to you at the end of the summer just before I go back to school."

> • Use words like "convenient" and "easy" and you will have soft, low-pressure closes.

Honesty

Ted surprised me that first day. He had made two sales out of four presentations and I was amazed at his quiet and gentle ease in closing the sales. On his fifth presentation, it appeared to me that the woman was about ready to buy. Then suddenly Ted packed up his books, thanked her for her courtesy and left. I asked him why he didn't close the sale. "She didn't need it," he replied. I felt I could have talked the woman into buying, but was impressed that Ted was satisfied and willing to let it go. He was always a perfect gentleman, a person of *honor and integrity*. He didn't need to close every single sale.

> • Ted Welch showed me how to be a master salesperson without pressure, without deceit and without tricks.

Service sales secrets

Let me tell you about another salesperson who *sells a lot of insurance without pressure*. I have been doing business with Herb Kristal for 30 years and would not consider buying my insurance from anyone else.

In fact, Herb has now retired and turned the business over to Steve Krochmal who is giving us the same kind of *low-pressure, high-service performance* that his mentor provided.

Herb and Steve both go to extraordinary lengths to do exhaustive research before they ever come to talk to me about my insurance. When they sit down with me, they talk to me about my needs, my finances, my goals and my dreams. The sales presentation is now merely a culmination of previous talks. We have already had a meeting of the minds and have reached *conceptual agreement* on what I need.

Thus, they do not have a one-plan-fits-all approach. They come to the presentation with a carefully-planned prospectus on *my* situation. It is very impressive, and by the time we are done, it is quite easy to say "yes." *No pressure, just excellence.* I have used them for business insurance as well as personal insurance. I have devoted an entire chapter to them later in the book.

Finding the right person

One of my *"Savage"* businesses was a school fund raising company called IFS. My two partners were Mike Rippey and Dennis Snyder. The three of us always stayed "in the trenches" calling on schools, even after we had built up a sales force of over 200 people.

We had a line of fashion jewelry with prices ranging from $3 to $20. We had an excellent brochure and a highly-motivating prize program. Schools that sold our jewelry made lots of money.

Back in the early days, when it was just the three of us, we discovered that the worst person to talk to in a high school was the principal. If we talked to the principal, the response was always the same: "Great idea. Leave your card. If anyone is interested, we will give you a call." Of course, no one ever called.

But who needed the money? In the high schools, it was usually the band or one of the athletic teams. So whom did we go see? Of course! The band director! Or the coach!

Now, here is how we *closed the sale without pressure*: we did *not* try to get the band director to say, "Yes, we will do it." We would show the band director the program and talk about how much the band would earn. We talked about how quick and easy it was. But then, instead of saying, "Do you want to do it?" we would say, "Most band directors like me to show it to the kids to see what they think. What time is band practice?

> * Would it be more convenient if I stopped by today or would tomorrow be better?"

When we showed it to the kids, they always liked it and the band director got excited. Usually, they started the sale that very same day. We had enormous success.

> * The key is to find the person who is motivated.

If you are selling a product that is going to be used by the plant manager, go see that person. Don't go to the purchasing manager. The purchasing manager will be just like the school principal. You will hear, "Leave your card and I'll call you back."

Yes, we often went to see the principal—but only *after* we had an appointment to "show it to the kids." Then, we would say to the principal, "Bob Band Director asked me to stop by tomorrow to talk to the kids about a possible fund raising project and I just wanted to make sure it didn't conflict with anything on your schedule." Notice, we were *not* asking for permission. By keeping it low-keyed and casual, we usually got the job done.

The same thing applies to the purchasing manager. If Tom, the plant manager, is excited about your product, he may be able to order it from you directly. That is the ideal situation. If not, you ask him, "How many do you want? When do you need them?" Then go to the purchasing manager and say, "I was just talking with Tom. He feels that my shrink wrap would be perfect for his canisters coming off the production line. He wants to order 1,000 cases as an initial order and wanted me to *check with you to see if he can get them in this month's budget or next month's.*" (Choice of "yes" or "yes.")

Choice of "yes" or "yes"

You will notice we have already discussed the choice of "yes" or "yes" a couple of times. This is one of the best ways for you to teach your salespeople how to *close a sale without pressure.*

Men's suit

I was buying a suit at Louis Boston, one of the finest and most unique men's clothing stores in America. I wanted a Giorgio Armani suit and was disappointed to find out they did not carry Armani clothing. However, I was open-minded to *anything Italian.* They had over a dozen Italian brands, plus some gorgeous Brioni ties. I was planning to spend $2,500 to $3,000 on a suit. The salesperson asked me about my business. I told him I was a public speaker and consultant. "Yes!" he said. *"I have several good choices for you."*

He knew my budget was in the $2,500 to $3,000 range, so he showed me a couple of suits in that range. They were beautiful. But then he pulled out a rich-looking fabric, an elegant suit crafted by Gianluca Isaia Napoli. I had not heard of the brand, but felt the material, caressed the material and immediately wanted it. Let me modify that. I wanted it *badly.* The salesperson said, "You would look fantastic in this suit when you give a speech."

How much?" I asked.

"$4,300."

I gulped. I stared longingly at the extraordinary cloth, first-rate construction, workmanship, style and fit. There it was: *my choice of "yeses."* I chose the $4,300 suit. But if that had been my ONLY choice, I would have walked out of the store.

> • Irony: After all that, I did a Guerrilla Marketing seminar in Dubai with Jay Levinson and wore an $18 "guerrilla" camouflage T-Shirt with my $4,300 suit!

Perfume sales secrets

I worked as sales and marketing consultant with Zermat, a perfume company in Mexico. It is a direct marketing company with a sales force of independent dealers, mostly women, similar to the structure at Avon.

> • My "Savage" technique as a sales consultant is the same as it has always been as a sales manager:
> • Get out in the trenches.

I went out and made sales calls with some of the "Zermat ladies." The best ones used the "yes or yes" technique all the time and I taught them a few additional ones. Then I met with the sales managers and the CEO and we established the following *"yes or yes" closing techniques that were all low pressure.*

- Do you prefer this fragrance or this one?
- Would you rather pay by cash or check?
- Do you like a spray or do you prefer direct application?
- I can come once a month or once every two months. What is more convenient for you?

And finally, after they had placed an order, they would always ask for a few referrals. This was also a choice of "yeses."

- You probably have a few friends who would like to know about these great perfumes. Which ones would be the best ones for me to visit?

Use low pressure to get high productivity from salespeople

We have talked about low pressure with the customers. Now let's talk about *low pressure with your salespeople.* You as sales manager can get great productivity from your salespeople by making them feel light-hearted, not tense. *Traditional sales managers* put pressure on their sales people and *operate on the basis of guilt. Savage Sales Managers* put enthusiasm into their sales people and *operate on the basis of joy.*

Let's go back to my sales manager, Ted Welch. He always made me feel good, even when I was having a tough time. One week I was #1 in the company and he congratulated me with great enthusiasm. The next week, I called him in a panic on Monday at 4 PM and told him I hadn't sold anything all day. Ted started to laugh. Then he laughed some more. In his slow, soft Tennessee drawl, he said,

> • "Steve, you're trying too hard. Just forget about sales.
> Just go out there, relax and visit with the folks."

That's the best advice he could have given me. A traditional sales manager would have put pressure on me to work harder, to try harder and to close more sales. Ted realized I was pushing myself to repeat my #1 performance of the previous week. He got me off the hook by laughing and getting me to relax.

Savage Sales Secret #2

Convert everyone in your company into a "Savage Salesperson"—even the accountants!

Let me tell you the story of Bob Aga. Bob was a teacher at a middle school in Richmond, California. We had a school fund raising company. Schools sold our products and earned money on each sale. Students won prizes. We made a profit on each product. Everybody won.

Most schools sold about $7,000 and kept $2,300 in profit. They paid us $4,700. That was our "wholesale" number.

Bob Aga volunteered to coordinate the fund raising program at his school. He was a history teacher and an all-around good guy. He helped out just because he wanted to help the school and help the kids. Because of his inspiration and organization, the school sold five times more than the average: $25,000 wholesale!

Mike, Dennis and I were thrilled and amazed. This was a huge boost for our small company. At that point, the three of us were still doing most of the selling. We had only four salespeople besides ourselves. (We would eventually grow to 250 salespeople.)

We called Bob and asked him to come in for a visit. We said, "Bob, you did an amazing job on your program. That is the most any school has sold. You are the kind of person that we want to have working in our company. How would you like to become a full-time sales representative with our company? We will call you our Fund Raising Director."

Bob was pleased with the offer, but demurred. He said, "Guys, I appreciate the offer, but my heart is in the school. I love teaching and I love the kids. This is my career."

We asked Bob what he was earning. Then we asked, "Bob, what if you could continue to work with kids and earn four times what you are earning right now?"

Two weeks later, Bob was calling on schools as a full-time Fund Raising Director!

Conflict between salespeople and office staff

Bob was so excited about his new job that he would come into the office every day after school was out to tell everybody about his results that day. School got out at 3:00 PM. Our offices and plant closed at 5:00 PM. Bob had two hours to go around and talk to everyone, from our controller to our plant manager to our customer service people. He bubbled over with joy every afternoon.

One day our controller, Bernard, came to me and said, "Steve, you've got to slow Bob down. He comes in every day and talks to everyone in the office. We don't have time for him. We are up to our necks in work. Tell him to stay away."

You can imagine Bernard, the controller. Grim, serious, business-like, a total numbers guy. When he smiled, his lips pointed down. He was a great controller and kept us three *"savages"* organized, but he did not like salespeople!

I replied, "Bernard, I appreciate your hard work and I don't want anyone wasting your time. However, I don't have the heart to tell Bob to stay away. He is doing a fantastic job, he's selling a lot, he's full of enthusiasm and he feels like we are one big happy family. I don't want to destroy that feeling."

Bernard grunted his disapproval.

Then I said, "I tell you what. Let's make a deal. Instead of having Bob come into the office, why don't you and all the other managers go out with Bob and call on our customers? You would go out for just half a day and you would get a much better sense of what our business is all about. That way Bob will have the feeling that we care about him and you will have a better idea of what our customers are thinking."

Bombshell! Thud.

Bernard did not like that idea at all. "No way! I'm too busy. I'm putting in 10 or 12 hours a day. I can't spare any time to go out and visit those crazy customers with that fanatical salesman!"

Mike, Dennis and I were all sales oriented. We had all sold books with the Southwestern Company and had the Ted Welch/Spencer Hays philosophy. We believed that our salespeople were our most important element. Back at the Southwestern Company, all the managers, even the accountants, had worked their way through college selling books, so they all shared in the same corporate philosophy. But we were a brand new company, and we had to convert corporate people to our way of thinking.

We had a weekly staff meeting. Bernard, our dour controller, was there. Arlene, our human resources director and Tom, our operations director, also attended. We three partners had to convince the other three people that they should also become "*savages*" and get out in the trenches with the salespeople. We had hired them from large corporations because we were young "*savages*" and we needed their executive experience. They had a lot to give to us. But we also had a lot to give to them.

How to convince managers to get "out in the trenches"

I wanted to sell them on the idea, not pressure them into it. So, I tried the old "soft" sell tactic. I began, "Mike, Dennis and I continue to go out in the field with our salespeople two days each week, no matter what the demands are here in the office. We think it is vital for us to keep our eyes and ears open so we know what is going on in our market. We want to hear what our customers are saying. We want to know our salespeople intimately.

"We would like you to consider going out with our salespeople for one half day. Just try it and see what you think. If you think it was useful, then you may want some of the managers and supervisors that work under you to do the same thing."

Arlene was enthusiastic about the idea and immediately agreed. Tom did not seem terribly excited but nodded his head. Bernard, who had already told me "no," grunted in dismay. He knew he was beaten.

To make sure it happened, we immediately scheduled each one of them for the next three days, half a day each. There was no getting out of it now!

I asked them to come and give me some feedback as soon as they got back. Tom was the first. He came back positively radiant. I had never seen him so excited. He said, "Steve, *those four hours changed my whole perspective on our business.* I saw how our customers react to our products and I saw mistakes my people had made in packing and shipping. We will correct those immediately. Also, I saw how hard Bob works and I have new respect for him. We got to know each other better as we drove from school to school and I understand why he gets so enthusiastic about the service we are providing the schools."

Arlene came in the next day. She was always upbeat, so I was not surprised when she told me how much she had enjoyed the day. But she had also learned something. As director of human resources, *she got a picture of how lonely a salesperson can feel,* and how detached from the company life can be when one is out in the field. In the office, everyone is together and she could create her magic sense of teamwork. She now wanted to give that same sense to the salespeople.

Finally it was the turn of Bernard, the stern controller. He had not been looking forward to this day. But he managed to get out there at 7:30 AM, when the school day began, and started making calls with good old Bob.

When Bernard reported back to me that afternoon, a dramatic change had come over him. The first thing I noticed was his smile. Those lips that used to point downward in a grimace were suddenly pointed upward in a genuine smile! Bernard looked happy! He acknowledged, "Well, Steve, I can't believe it, but I actually had a good time. It's a different world out there. I saw Bob get up in front of 200 kids. He showed them the products and the prizes—and they were actually screaming like they were at a concert. It was really fun. At another school, the teacher showed us her invoice and the computer printout. She was confused by a few things on it. I immediately saw a few things we could do to make it simpler and easier for her."

After that, we quickly scheduled a time when each manager and supervisor, as well as each customer service person, would spend half a day riding around with either Bob or one of our other Fund Raising Directors. Now that we had the three top people convinced, it was easy for them to convince those that reported to them.

> • After everyone had spent a half-day in the field, we decided to make this part of our corporate philosophy. Everyone would spend one half-day in the field every six months.

This became an article of faith with the company. We would insist that it be put on the calendar at the beginning of each six-month period. This was the most sacrosanct appointment of the entire six months. Nothing was allowed to interfere. You could not get out of it by saying, "I'm too busy" or "I have a meeting."

Corporate culture change sales secrets

What were the results of this strategy? The company became much more vibrant and customer-oriented. It had started out as three "Mom-and-Pop: operations. My wife Barrie and I had started in our garage. Dennis and Mike had started with their wives in their garages. When we were barely surviving, we did whatever it took to make the customers happy. Now, with an ever-growing staff, we needed to maintain that same enthusiasm and flavor.

> • No matter how big we got, we resolved to retain that "Mom and Pop" spirit.

Our sales grew because teachers, coaches, band directors and PTA presidents loved us. The reason they loved us was because they got great service from customer service people who could talk to them intelligently—since they knew what it was like out there in the schools.

They also loved us because they got great products that were well packaged, since our production people had been out there to see how the products arrived.

They also loved us because our invoices and tabulation of each student's orders were so simple and easy to understand, since our accounting and computer people had been out there to see how the customers read and interpreted those statements.

Our company established the reputation of being "easy to do business with," an issue we will develop in detail in Chapter Five.

And our sales grew, doubling each year, until we reached $60 million in six years and sold it to Colgate-Palmolive.

The urgency of changing your corporate culture

Traditional companies stagnate or die. Companies that change are *Savages*. Here are some of the changes that I have helped companies confront in my years as a sales consultant, often working in Latin America. I was fortunate to grow up in Ecuador, the son of missionary parents, so am grateful to be 100% bi-lingual. Thus, many of my examples will be from Latin America. But they are equally valid in the United States or any other country.

From production to marketing sales secrets

I worked as a consultant with a ceramics company in Ecuador. They had a sales force of 60 people that covered the entire country. Until about 20 years ago, they had a near-monopoly on the ceramics business in the beautiful nation of 13,500,000 people.

Then came competition, first from the neighboring countries of Peru and Colombia, which was serious, then from China and Thailand, which was deadly. New designs, lower prices. The company had to change its strategy. That's when they called on me.

After spending a few days "in the trenches" with their salespeople (which I always do when I start a new assignment), I sat down with the owner of the company to analyze what was happening. Here is what I told him:

> - "In the past, you were a production company.
> - People bought what you produced.
> - *Now you need to look at yourselves as a marketing company.*
> - *You must produce what people want.*"

They had an efficient plant and made good products. But some of the products were out of date and people no longer wanted them. They had to bite the bullet and throw away some of their favorite molds. But when they listened to the market, their sales began to increase, they were able to compete with the Chinese, and they returned to profitability.

For you to be a great *Savage Sales Manager,* you need to work with your production people, not just with your sales people. You need to make sure your production people understand the market and that they are producing what people want and need.

You need to sell them on the idea of thinking like salespeople. Do it in an upbeat and friendly way. Don't do it in a conflictive way. Traditional companies have a constant turf war going on between sales and production. A *Savage Company* recognizes that there is a natural tendency for a conflict to grow between sales and production people, and must do everything possible to avoid it.

You must be a sales manager to your production people just like you are to your sales people. Thank them for their work. Congratulate them for their quality. Praise them for getting the job done.

Most of all, you need to make sure they are producing what people want and need. This requires constant coordination with marketing, production and sales. You are all on the same team. Don't fight.

- No turf wars for savages.
- We work together and we get the job done.
- Convert your production people into happy partners—sales production savages.

From monopoly to competition sales secrets

I did a *Savage Sales Seminar* in Spanish in El Salvador. Several people were from one of the large telephone companies.

After the seminar, the manager talked to me and said, "Steve, we used to be the only company in El Salvador. We had a complete monopoly. We could do whatever we wanted. Then the cell phones came in under our noses. Later, the government broke up our monopoly. Now there are two major telephone companies, plus several cell phone companies. It is a mad house. Your *Savage Sales Seminar* helped us see how we could do many things at no cost at all. We have proven that these techniques work—even for a large company like ours."

A few weeks later, she sent me an email and said, "It was incredible, but when we did not have a budget to launch a new product for land lines and voice mail, we decided to think of all the ways you had taught us that we could promote the product without any cost at all, and that is when our creativity flowed more than ever before.

"We made visits to 23 radio stations, conducted a press conference for all the media, sent emails to all the clients and all the employees of our company, text messages and demonstrations of our service to our commercial agencies. Just doing that, we have gained 34,150 new clients in one month. Our original projection was 40,000 clients in three months! Thank you for all your great ideas."

Your role as a *Savage Sales Manager* is to get your team together and get them to think creatively. Think of ways they can do things at low cost without spending a fortune. Low budget, or better yet, free. This means that you engage not only the sales people but the folks in the office and the plant. Make them all part of the *Savage Squad*.

To be a great *Savage Sales Manager* means that you have to think expansively. You don't limit yourself to thinking about managing your group of salespeople. You think of doing whatever it takes to provide your salespeople with the weapons they need to make them successful. Thus, you are constantly on the move inside the corporate hallways, making everyone feel like salespeople, from the accountants to the computer techs. Treat them like heroes, just like you treat your salespeople.

If you are working with a large corporation like the telephone company mentioned above, you have to work harder than ever to avoid the classic turf wars that go on in most large companies. You can convert your company into a *Savage Operation* by making sure that everyone becomes a *Savage Salesperson*. It may sound corny, but believe me, as they become accustomed to the idea, they will love it.

From bureaucracy to effective agility

Even a small company can become bureaucratic. I told you earlier how we maintained the "Mom and Pop" spirit at IFS, our school fund raising company. But it was not always easy, even after we launched our campaign to have everyone spend one half day "in the trenches" once every six months.

Anna was our customer service manager. She was in her early 20's but had maturity beyond her years. She was bubbling with enthusiasm, smart and dynamic. Under her leadership, our customer service department quickly grew to three, then ten and eventually forty customer service representatives. She was magnificent.

We had grown to ten customer service reps. They were doing a terrific job. But I noticed that Anna was asking me way too many questions. I didn't mind, because she was so pleasant and fun to be around. However, she wasn't making decisions. She was asking me for permission way too often. I didn't get it at first, but one day it dawned on me what was happening.

We sat down and talked about it. I said, "Anna, you are just as smart as I am. You have been out in the schools. You are on the phone every day talking to schools. You know our customers. And you know our company. I want you to make all the decisions. You don't need to consult me. Just decide. I'll back you up on any decision."

Anna looked pleased, but a little concerned.

"What if I make the wrong decision?"

"Anna, I make wrong decisions too! That's how we learn. If you don't decide and make a few mistakes, you'll never grow. Just decide. Usually you'll be right. And if you're wrong, I'll never get mad at you. You will have my full support."

She pondered that for awhile and then grinned from ear to ear. "I like it!" She jumped up and went to work.

After a few weeks I noticed that the customer service reps were doing the same thing to Anna as she had been doing to me. They were asking her to make a lot of decisions. She was great, and her decisions were sound.

> - A customer hates to hear, "Let me speak with my manager."
> - *The customer wants a decision, **now**.*

So we all got together. I said, "A few weeks ago, I told Anna to start making decisions on her own, without consulting me. She's been doing great and we're both happy. But now I want each of you to have the same power and the same freedom. Your customers will love you if you can make intelligent decisions immediately, without consulting anyone.

We then had a discussion in which each representative shared the types of decisions they were afraid to make on their own.

Peggy said, "One customer refused to pay our $50 shipping charge. I asked Anna if we could write it off. She gave me the OK."

I asked, "How much did the school sell?"

"$4,000."

I said, "Peggy, if this were your business, and a school bought $4,000 from you, would you be willing to write off a $50 shipping charge in order to make that school happy?"

"Absolutely!"

"Well, that's your answer!" I replied. "Think of this as your company. Make a decision that's good for the customer and good for the company. But if you have any doubt, tilt in favor of the customer."

Then I asked them to give me a worst-case scenario.

Sandy told me about a school band that ordered $6,000 worth of fashion jewelry. Then after they received the shipment the school board suddenly decided that there would be no more fund raising for the rest of the school year. She had asked Anna what to do about it.

Again, I asked Sandy the same question, "What would you do if it were your own business?"

"I'd take it back."

"Would you be mad?"

"Yes, but I wouldn't let the customer know I was mad."

"Do you think that band director will do business again with us next year?"

"Yes, he was so pleased that I did not give him a hard time about it. But it would have been better if I had given him an immediate decision instead of consulting Anna and calling him back."

"OK, Sandy," I said. "There's your answer. Think of this as your business. And think long range. Don't think only about this year's business. Think about next year. *Think about how you can make this customer a happy customer forever and ever.* Make your decision based on that philosophy and you can always give your customer an immediate decision, right now, on the phone, without consulting anyone."

The customer service people loved their new power. Our customers loved us. And our business continued to grow.

We also had weekly (sometimes daily) discussions in which we talked about situations that had come up during the week. We made sure the salespeople out in the field had a chance to interact with our customer service representatives so everyone had input.

> - Every salesperson and every customer service representative developed a common corporate culture.
> - *We were all on the same team, building the company, by making the customer the hero.*
> - This was not just a slogan; it was the way we operated.

Savage Sales Secret #3

Convert your sales force into "savage beasts of productivity"

This next "*Savage Sales Secret*" is designed to discover and release the untamed fury inside your salespeople. I have trained and managed thousands of salespeople—and the biggest surprises were those who were not the smooth-talking, glib, charming, "natural" sales types. The champions often turned out to be the quiet, shy, reserved people with an inner reserve of power that was unleashed once we turned them loose on the field of battle.

Ken Snyder – a physically impaired sales champion

Ken Snyder was a fellow student of mine at Wheaton College. He was nearly blind. People liked him, but he was kind of reserved because he could not see very well. Thus, he did not make friends easily. He was a serious student and a serious person. No one would have ever dreamed that Ken was cut out to be a salesperson.

At the end of his sophomore year, Ken was offered an opportunity to sell books door-to-door with Southwestern Company. No one expected him to do a great job. In fact, we wondered how he would find his way around, due to his serious problems with his vision. We knew he would work hard, but we wondered if he would last more than a couple of weeks.

We all went to Nashville, Tennessee, for five days of sales training. We were taught the cycle of selling, which included the approach, presentation and close. Most of all, we were trained to keep a positive mental attitude.

We were all given the classic book ***How I Raised Myself from Failure to Success in Selling*** by Frank Bettger and were asked to read it. We got motivational speeches every day. We were told that the most important thing was "not to quit." "Whatever you do, boys, don't quit." (Yes, we were all college *boys* back in 1959. I will tell you more about that later on!) A theme throughout was *"Winners never quit. And quitters never win."*

Despite all that, about 10% of the sales force quit the first week. It was a grueling, tough job. Rejection was severe. We called on 30 people a day. If we were good, we made 20 demonstrations a day and sold 7 or 8 books. A lot of guys made 10 demonstrations a day and sold 2 or 3 books. And a lot of guys quit. By the end of that summer, approximately 40% had quit.

Well, Ken was not a quitter. He could not see very well, but he could knock on doors. And he knew his sales talk. Instead of calling on 30 people a day, he called on 50 a day. Instead of 20 demonstrations a day, he made 35. Instead of 8 sales, he made 15. By the end of the summer, he was number one among all the first year salesmen.

The next summer, Ken was a student manager. Most guys came back the second summer with a team of 3 or 4 students. They got paid a percentage on the production of each person on their team. Ken had 20 students on his team. He finished up the summer as the number one salesman and the number one student manager.

Ken was the perfect example of the importance of giving a person a chance who may not be your model of the ideal salesperson. He had that "inner fury" and the Southwestern Company helped him realize his potential, turning him into a "wild beast of productivity."

Often a person with a handicap will be a powerful salesperson. No one ever felt sorry for Ken. They simply admired him. He was able to attract 20 people to join him the second summer because his story was so compelling. He did not have to give them a glib sales talk. He simply said, "If you go out there this summer and follow my example, work 12 hours a day, make 35 demonstrations a day, for 12 weeks, all summer, you will be successful." They followed his example and he developed other successful salespeople.

Ken's third summer was even more amazing. Many of his 20 salespeople came back with their own teams. Thus, he had an organization with about 100 students. And by the fourth summer, he had over 200 students in his organization, at the time the largest student organization in the 100-year history of the Southwestern Company.

He continued to be a good student at Wheaton College even while he was working hard recruiting, developing and training his student managers throughout his college years. His qualities of toughness, tenacity, and stick-to-itiveness were admirable. He graduated from college with plenty of money in the bank. Most of all, he graduated with confidence in himself, assured that he would be able to face any obstacle in life and conquer whatever came his way.

- As a sales manager, you should always be looking for the person who has that inner grit, that steely determination and drive to succeed.
- Often a sales job will allow that person show what he or she can do.

The Snyder brothers

Ken Snyder had two younger brothers, Ralph and Dennis. His second summer, part of his 20-man crew was his younger brother, Ralph. Ken had the disability of poor vision. Ralph had his own disability: he was very shy. He was lovable and friendly, but always bashful. People had to approach him to strike up a friendship. Who would have ever dreamed that Ralph would make it in sales?

Well, his older brother Ken *knew* he could. "Ralph, if I can do it, anyone can do it. All you have to do is follow my example and do what I do. Can you knock on 30 doors a day?"

"Yes," Ralph replied warily.

Will you work 13 hours a day, even when it's raining?"

"Yes."

"If people slam the door in your face, are you going to quit?"

"No."

"Will you learn your sales talk and give it word-for-word?"

"Yes."

"OK, brother, let's go."

Ralph, for all his timidity, followed his brother's lead and finished #8 among the 1500 first-year salesmen.

Next it was the turn of the youngest Snyder brother, Dennis. After seeing the success of his two older brothers, he could not resist the call and joined the team immediately after graduation from high school. He was determined to begin his freshman year in college with money in the bank.

Dennis was neither blind nor shy. He was a bundle of enthusiasm and everyone was sure he would succeed. But deep down inside, he was afraid. His two brothers had been a huge success and now enormous expectations were placed upon his shoulders. But he followed the same formula his brother had laid on Ralph. Thirty visits a day. Thirteen hours a day, positive mental attitude and follow the time-tested sales talk word-for-word.

By the end of the summer, Dennis ranked precisely where Ralph had ended: number eight first-year salesman among 1,500 college students! (Note: All guys. More on this later!) The Snyder boys had become a Southwestern legend.

Three years later, I became a full-time sales manager with Southwestern and inherited Dennis Snyder as part of my organization. What a trip! We recruited together at Westmont College in Santa Barbara, California. It is a small college with about 1400 students and Dennis spread the word about the wonderful opportunities afforded by the Southwestern Company. I visited the campus several times and Dennis always had a group of students primed for the interview. He was among the best organized of all my student managers.

By June, 17 guys had joined Dennis' team and took the trip east from California to Tennessee. Notice I said "guys." This was 1968 and Southwestern Company was still an "all guy's sales force." But 1968 was a very special year. One woman joined the sales force that summer. I will tell Cheryl's story in the next chapter. Meanwhile, let's stick to the story of Dennis Snyder and his 17 guys from Westmont College.

They drove from Santa Barbara, California to Nashville, Tennessee. Then they went through the greatest five-day sales school in America. After that, they drove to Atlanta, the territory I had reserved for Dennis and his team. We wanted them to be as far away from home as possible to keep them focused on the job and to make it harder for them to quit and go home.

What would we normally expect from a team of 17 guys? A typical team would have about 10% "quitters" the first week. It is an extremely difficult job and the rejection is simply too much to bear for a lot of college kids. So, we would have expected about 2 of Dennis' guys to quit after the first week. Naturally, we never said this out loud. We talked constantly about the virtues of perseverance and the character building that came with sticking it out for twelve weeks, no matter how tough the situation.

But at the end of week one, all 17 of Dennis' team were still working.

By the end of the summer, it was not unusual to have lost about 30% to 40% of the team. Therefore, we would have expected Dennis to have about 10-12 guys left at the end of August. But guess what? All 17 of them finished the summer, came through Nashville, picked up their checks, and drove back to California, feeling successful.

I asked Dennis how he did it.

- We made a commitment to each other before we left California.
- *We agreed among ourselves that we're gonna do it, we're gonna make money and we're gonna be special.*
- That was our mantra.
- There was a lot of peer pressure not to fail.

"We also felt kind of isolated since we were from the West Coast. Most of the salespeople were from the Midwest and the South. This made us feel kind of different, even arrogant.

The "BMOC" syndrome

You may be surprised that the person who was the *"Big Man on Campus"* will often fall on his face in selling. I used to be amazed when this would happen. I would interview a person who was handsome, charming, talkative and persuasive. I would sign him up on the spot, enthusiastic and optimistic, convinced that this person would succeed. Often, of course, he or she would succeed. But sometimes it just didn't work.

Why not?

The BMOC is not used to rejection. A guy who is handsome and has an easy time getting dates is stunned when a customer says "no." A guy who is not so good-looking and has gotten rejected all his life is not surprised when a customer says "no." Rejection is something he can handle!

Olga in Monterrey

Another example of a person who was not a "natural" salesperson joined my sales force in Mexico. One of my sales operations took me to the bustling city of Monterrey, in northern Mexico. We had recruited salespeople all over Mexico, in all 31 states, and I had visited all of them. But we had somehow failed to find a person to make it in Monterrey, the third largest city in Mexico with the highest per capita income. We had hired three people, all men, all promising, with good personalities and good resumes. But they did not hit their sales targets and the company had to terminate them.

On this trip, I interviewed Olga, a 55-year-old housewife. She was pleasant, but rather ordinary looking. She did not quite fit the "profile" of the company, but I could detect her inner passion and drive. She told me, "Give me a chance. I will show you what I can do."

I recommended that we hire Olga. The regional sales manager was skeptical. He wanted someone younger and, quite frankly, prettier. But I asked him to let me work with Olga and give us a chance. He agreed, without enthusiasm.

Well! Olga's inner fury was released. She drove the younger people (men and women!) into the shadows with her outstanding performance. Her intensity and passion for success gave her an outstanding work ethic. She worked harder and longer than anyone else. The customers loved her because she was down-to-earth and "just like one of them." Within six months, she was number one in the company.

The lesson for you, as a sales manager, is this: Don't be deceived by pretty looks and smooth talk. Yes, a beautiful person can be very successful and an eloquent talker can be a terrific salesperson.

- Don't overlook the quiet and the shy.
- There are inner reservoirs of strength that have built up inside these folks.
- Tap into them.
- Give them a chance.
- You will be glad you did.

Savage Sales Secret #4

The profile of the ideal salesperson

What does not matter

Experience in sales does not matter

Many of the most successful people I have ever hired had no experience in sales when they started out. When we started our school fund raising company, our first inclination was to hire experienced salespeople. We did, and we had success with some of them. But we had our greatest success with principals, band directors and coaches. These were people that knew the school's environment and were leaders. They were also underpaid and overworked. They were glad to stay in the school environment and make a lot more money!

Jim was a football coach in Michigan. He had no experience in sales. But he had a lot of experience in motivating and inspiring people. We hired him as a Fund Raising Director with IFS. He knew how to build a winning football team. Those skills made him a winner as a salesperson. Within a year, we asked him to become a sales manager. He was in charge of 12 other salespeople, just like a football team. In this case, he was a player-coach, because he continued to sell in his own territory. Within 5 years, he became vice president of sales, in charge of the Central Region of the United States.

Jim was not a flashy salesperson. The qualities that made him successful as a coach were his low-keyed, honest, solid communication with his players combined with a strong work ethic. He approached our customers with the same droll, slow, believable approach. They trusted and liked him. They wanted to do business with him.

When he became a sales manager, the other Fund Raising Directors looked up to him because he always did more than he asked them to do. If he asked them to call on the first school at 7:30 AM, he would call on his first school at 7:00 AM. If he told them to stay out in the field until 4:30 PM, he would stay out until 5:00 PM. They knew he was putting in those hours, because they would ride around with him and watch him work. He led by example. He did not need to give orders. He just showed them how to do it.

Age does not matter

Howard was 68 when he joined our sales force. He had been a successful high school principal and a college president. He had never sold a product, but he had sold education to thousands of young people. He did not consider it beneath his dignity to go out and call on schools and sell them on the idea of doing a fund raising program with our company. He was enthusiastic and sincere.

At age 68, he was still full of incredible energy. He was not interested in sitting back and retiring. He wanted to keep busy and continue to be productive. He moved so fast that we quickly asked him to become a trainer. When we sent young salespeople to work with Howard, they would report back that he would often leave them breathless, walking faster than they were used to, often lagging 10 or 20 steps behind!

Among the thousands of salespeople I have trained, some of the most productive have been those over 65. As a sales manager, you should be alert and open to men and women who have been forced to leave their companies just because of the artificial retirement age of 65. In many cases, they are financially secure, but simply want to keep working for their own higher goals and objectives. In other cases, the pension plans do not provide them the same standard of living they were used to, and they really need the money. In either case, you will find them to be a highly motivated group of people—and you should be wide open in seeking them for your sales force.

Gender does not matter

When I was a college student working with the Southwestern Company, it was an all-boys' company. This was back in 1960, the dark ages in terms of opportunities for women. There were about 2,000 students (guys) who sold books door-to-door every summer. I worked for five summers. After the first summer, I built a team each summer. I was a student manager and made a commission on the sales of my team. At the same time, I continued to work full-time as a salesman.

After college, I became a full-time sales manager with Southwestern. My territory was vast, from Illinois to California. One of my student managers was Dave at the University of Kansas. Dave was looking for a team of "men" to mentor and train that summer. We had a conference room at the student center. Dave brought five young men to the interview. He also brought his girlfriend, Cheryl.

Cheryl sat back in the corner while I interviewed the guys. I told them all about the opportunities to make a lot of money. However, most of my interview focused on the incredible experience they would have—going to another part of the country, meeting and dealing with people, learning how to cope with hundreds of unforeseen situations and becoming a stronger person. We talked a lot about personal growth and development. We talked about how this experience would help them get better jobs when they graduated.

The young men were impressed. Three out of five signed a dealer agreement to participate. All five left the room.

Then Dave, Cheryl and I talked about the candidates and analyzed each of them. Suddenly Cheryl spoke up. "Steve, I can do that!"

I was startled. "Cheryl, I am sure you could, but this job is for guys."

(Remember, these were the Dark Ages, back in 1969, and things were different for women!)

- Cheryl replied, calmly,
- "Steve, give me a chance. I'll show you what I can do."

I said, "Well, Cheryl, it's gonna be tough. You have mean people. You have doors slammed in your face. You have to work long hours. Dogs will bite you. You have lots of rejection. It's a horrible job." (This was a role reversal for me! Usually I was trying to talk guys into taking the job. Now I was trying to talk Cheryl out of it!)

Cheryl insisted. "Steve, I can do it! Just let me try."

I could not resist. I said, "Ok, let's keep it a secret. Just go out there and see what you can do!"

We had a Gold Award for every salesman that worked 12 ½ hours a day, 6 days a week, 75 hours a week, for 12 weeks. Cheryl went beyond the Gold Award. She worked 80 hours a week all summer long. By the end of the summer, she was #3 among all the first-year salespeople.

It was not easy for Cheryl. It was not easy for a guy, but she had a lot more pressure on her to prove that a woman could do it. One day she sold $300—a stunning achievement back in those days. The next day, feeling under tremendous pressure to match her record day, she sold nothing at all. She called me in a panic. I laughed and I gave her the old Ted Welch advice: *"Just go out there and visit with the folks."* She calmed down and her sales quickly shot back up.

Back at the University of Kansas, when I was trying to talk her out of doing this, I had warned her that dogs would bite her. At the end of the summer she said, "Well, Steve, I didn't get bitten by any dogs, but I did get chased by a few." I also had warned her that someone might point a gun at her. That prediction came true. "Yes, Steve, I had a shotgun pointed at me along with some threats as I nervously walked to my car."

I asked Cheryl to share a few other memorable incidents from her dramatic summer. "One time I met a family in their yard and sold them a super set. When they went into the house to get their money,

I noticed a *No Soliciting* sign by the door. I would most likely have passed them by if I hadn't met them in their yard.

"Once I left the driveway of someone who did not buy and accidentally knocked over their mailbox. They came running out to make sure I wasn't hurt. I offered to pay for the mailbox. It wasn't hurt, just knocked over, and they were nice enough to refuse any payment."

Cheryl showed her dedication and determination to succeed during that magical summer of 1969 when the original Woodstock festival took place in New York. She was working in central New York State and was tempted to join the throng, but nothing could get in the way of her goals. She wanted to prove to everyone that a woman could be a success selling books door to door in an all-male world.

The Southwestern Company was never the same! Today there are still nearly 3,000 college students who sell books every summer—nearly half of whom are women.

> • My proudest achievement as a sales manager was to be the first to bring a woman into the sales ranks of a magnificent 100-year old publishing company.

My daughter, Cynthia, followed Cheryl into the "Book Field" 18 years later. Like Cheryl, Cynthia was #3 among the first-year salespeople. Nothing could have made me prouder. By the time Cynthia arrived, the Southwestern Company had a different corporate culture. It was no longer a male-dominated company. It not only had women salespeople, but many women in the ranks of sales managers as well as administrative managers throughout the company.

Cynthia was successful for the same reasons Cheryl was successful. She worked 80 hours a week, all summer long. She worked harder than most of the guys, and she beat the guys. She was powerful and persuasive. She was pretty and charming. But most of all, she was tough and gutsy, and refused to quit, even when she was discouraged.

One day, after Cynthia had been working for her first few weeks, with great initial success, she called me, weeping. She had worked all day and not made a single sale. The week before, she had received honors and accolades. She was under pressure (self-imposed) to keep it up. She was too tense and trying too hard.

As her Dad, I wanted desperately for her to succeed. My initial instinct was to tell her to go back out and work harder and try harder. Oh, how wrong that would have been!

Suddenly, I remembered the great advice I got from my own Sales Manager, Ted Welch, 30 years earlier, when I was in exactly the same predicament. Ted laughed. He laughed and I relaxed. So I did the same with Cynthia. *I laughed.* I told her the same thing had happened to me. I told her I had spent many hours on the book field, weeping!

> - I told her the same thing Ted Welch had told me 30 years earlier,
> - "Cynthia, you're trying too hard.
> - Just forget about sales.
> - Just go out there, *relax and visit with the folks.*"

She relaxed. She knew she was not alone. And her sales came back, easily, gracefully, until she became #3 first-year salesperson that summer. She made me mighty proud!

I pondered the magic of the number 3. I was #3 first-year salesperson back in 1960. Cheryl was #3 first-year salesperson in 1969. Cynthia was #3 salesperson in 1984. We all would have loved to be #1, but we were competing with mighty powerful folks and #3 was a terrific achievement.

Education does not matter

Yes, I'm all for education, and encourage everyone to go as far as they can. However, I have had success with people who did not even finish high school. As a sales manager, you should always be on the lookout for the person who is *self-educated*, who may not have had a chance to finish school, but who has persevered against all odds to become successful.

I owned a real estate appraisal company in New England for a few years. My son, Matt, got into the appraisal business and persuaded me to do it. He was in California. I was 3,000 miles away. All my good ideas came from him.

I hired several appraisers to work for me. Usually I required a college education. However, I interviewed Rob, who had only a high school education. He had passed his appraisal exams with high scores. He was well dressed and well groomed. He spoke with confidence and good vocabulary.

Part of his job as an appraiser was to sell. It was not enough to go out and appraise properties. Our appraisers had to call on mortgage companies and banks. This was a true selling job. Most appraisers did not know how to do it. This gave us a huge competitive edge and helped us build our company quickly into profitability.

Rob was diligent in all his appraisal courses. He was equally meticulous in preparing for his sales calls. He and I would work out his plan for the week, figuring out how many calls he would make per week, per day and per hour. We would map it all out so he would be completely efficient. He was enthusiastic and eager to make cold calls.

Here is how we got *high productivity without high pressure*:

We would walk into a bank or mortgage company and talk with the receptionist. It was very simple. "Hi, I'm Steve Savage. I'm an appraiser. I need to talk with your manager. Who is in charge of appraisals?"

By asking that question, we got directed to the right person. We also got the person's name.

> • We were selling, but it didn't sound like selling.

When we saw the manager, the pitch was very simple and low-keyed. "Hi, Sally. I'm Steve Savage. I'm an appraiser. I just wanted to check with you *real quick*. Are you getting pretty good turnaround on your appraisals?"

The phrase "*real quick*" got them relaxed. They knew they were not going to have a long, tedious sales pitch.

And the question about "turnaround" was powerful. The biggest complaint with most mortgage companies was that appraisers were too slow. When I asked that question, the manager usually said, "Hmm. Sit down. Whatcha got?"

We had a flyer with our address and logo. But the three key words were printed in big, bold type:

> # *Accurate!*
> # *Friendly!*
> # *Fast!*

We also had a flyer with testimonials from other mortgage companies who had done business with us. We handed that flyer to the manager. Then we simply said, "Would you give us a try?"

The answer was almost always, "Sure."

Then, we would ask, "As long as we are here, would you mind if we dropped off a flyer on the desk of each loan officer?"

Again, the answer was almost always, "OK."

Then we would go to each loan officer and give him or her the same short sales pitch. It was important for them to get our flyers and get to know us, because in most mortgage companies, the loan officers were able to choose their own appraisers.

- We had a *soft* approach, a *soft* presentation and a *soft* close.
- It worked.

Matt went beyond all these steps. He often took pizza to a mortgage company and ran a pizza party for all the loan officers. Sometimes he took wine. Occasionally, he took dessert. He was full of imagination. His idea was to do something different every time he visited the mortgage company. He visited each company over and over. They got to know and like him. When they needed an appraiser, they immediately thought of Matt.

> - *No high pressure.*
> - Just diligence, friendliness, follow-up, creativity, fun and consistent presence.
> - The result: *high productivity.*

Savage Sales Secret #5

Make your company easy

The radiator man

Mike was a successful salesman for a major auto parts manufacturer. For many years, he gave his time, energy, heart and soul to the company. He specialized in automobile radiators.

Mike saw several things the company was doing wrong, but he couldn't make them change. He was frustrated because he couldn't provide his customers with the service they needed. He knew he could do it better.

When a customer blew up a radiator, he or she needed a replacement fast. However, no radiator shop or garage could provide quick service. It took days to get a replacement or repair. And the supply of radiators at each shop was meager. With all the car models over the past 30 years, there were over 2000 different radiators to choose from. No radiator shop could afford to stock more than 30 or 40 different types.

Mike took a huge gamble. He quit his high-paying job and launched his own business. He rented a warehouse and made deals with dozens of radiator manufacturers all over the world. He stocked 1200 of the most common radiators. Then he went around to every garage in the area and told them he would guarantee delivery within one hour.

Garage owners were astonished. They had never replaced radiators before. They had always sent their customers to a radiator shop. But Mike showed them how they could make extra money by simply replacing a radiator, on the spot. Instead of spending $70 and waiting a few days for a repair, a customer could spend $120 and get a brand new radiator within an hour.

It was an imaginative move and Mike's business took off. He expanded his warehouses to other cities. His customers loved him.

Mike sold the business, became a multi-millionaire, and stayed with the new company as advisor.

> • What did it take?
> • An idea of how to do something better and a lot of guts.

Did it take a lot of money? Not much. Mike was able to get his suppliers to extend credit to him and thus started on a shoestring.

> • Make it easy for your customer.
> • You will dramatically out hustle your competitors.
> • You will build your business into a powerhouse.

Is your company easy? Think about it. Spy on yourself. Pretend you are a customer and call your company. See how easy it is to get information, to get through to the person you want, to buy something, to return a product or to get technical help. You may be in for a shock.

FedEx makes it easy

FedEx has always made it easy for its customers by giving power to its customer salespeople. From its earliest days, the customer service person had the power to make a quick decision, on the phone, without consulting a supervisor or manager. If there was any question about a shipment that got delayed, the customer service representative had the power to credit the customer's account.

I had a dramatic example of this a few years ago when I was doing a consulting job for a winery in Argentina. They shipped a case of wine to me by FedEx. I needed that case of wine to show at a wine tasting in Boston. No wine tasting, no wine sale.

The wine had been shipped in plenty of time, two weeks before the tasting. I should have had it three or four days after it got shipped. But a week went by and no wine. I called FedEx. The wine was held up in U.S. Customs in Memphis, Tennessee. We had clearly stated on the FedEx air bill that we would pay all customs duties. "Yes," said the FedEx person, "we are doing our best to clear it through customs."

I called every day, increasingly nervous and desperate. The wine did not arrive. The wine tasting came and went. The wine finally arrived two days after the event.

FedEx could easily have blamed U.S. Customs. The delay was not the fault of FedEx. They had done everything possible. But they did not hesitate. They gave me *full credit* for the shipment: $169. And the person that made the decision was not a supervisor or a manager. She was Lucille, the smart and friendly customer service rep who talked with me on the phone.

I have been a faithful and enthusiastic FedEx customer for 25 years. They have always treated me with this kind of first class service.

How does your company treat your customers? Do you bend over backwards to make things right for your customer, even when it means taking a temporary hit? Do you give your salespeople and your customer service people the power to make decisions, on the spot, so that your customers have a delightful and a positive experience with your company? If not, change your procedure immediately. Your company will be transformed.

From a difficult company to an easy company

Recently I did a consulting assignment for a chain of shoe stores. One day, I was standing in the corner of one of the stores, taking notes.

A well-dressed woman walked in with a box of shoes under her arm. She laid it on the counter. "My mother bought me a pair of shoes. They are one size too big. Would you replace these with the correct size?"

"Sure," said the clerk. "May I have your receipt?"

"Oh!" exclaimed the lady, "this was a gift from my mother. She lost the receipt."

The clerk was crestfallen. "Sorry, but no receipt, no return."

I was over in the corner freaking out. The woman's shoes in the right size were right in the window. An exchange would have been so simple.

Later, I talked to the CEO of the chain of stores. "Charlie, your company is not easy. You make it hard on the customer." I told him the story I just told you.

Charlie gave me a lame reply. "Customers take advantage. Who knows if she bought those shoes from us?"

I felt like screaming, but tried to stay calm. "Charlie, you're making it hard on everyone because you don't trust a few. Who cares if a few of them take advantage of you? What would it cost you? Nothing! Those shoes are on the shelves. Just replace them. 95% of your customers are honest. You want to make them feel like you are friendly and you trust them. Why don't we do a test? Let's put a sign on the door of one of your stores saying 'We cheerfully accept exchanges.' Let's try it for 6 months. Then let's compare it with your other stores."

Charlie was skeptical. But he tried it. That store's sales increased 16% while the other stores were flat. The company's culture was transformed.

The sign was not terribly significant, because not that many people needed to return a pair of shoes. But it conveyed an attitude of friendliness and trust.

- It made the employees feel like owners.
- The employees felt good about working for the company.
- The customers felt good about doing business there.
- That is why sales went up.

Savage Sales Secret #6

Make your company exciting for your salespeople

Our goal in this book is for everyone in the company to think and act like a salesperson. The theme of "*Savage Sales Secrets*" is to get everyone on the same wavelength so that anyone who contacts the company will feel treated like royalty.

If the in-house employees are happy, the outside sales force will have more success. If they are successful, sales will grow and the company will prosper. Thus, it is in everyone's interest to make sure that sales are the driving force that guide and motivate the company.

Happy employees = happy clients.

Making your employees happy is not just a nice sentiment. It is good business. Traditional companies operate on the basis of guilt and punishment. Savage companies operate on the basis of congratulations and excitement.

Who is the most important person in the company? The CEO? Think again! Who is the person that the customer usually contacts when they call the company? The receptionist! Yes, the receptionist in the most important person in the company for the average customer. But, sadly, the receptionist is usually one of the lowest paid people with the lowest prestige…at most traditional companies.

But a "*Savage Company*" is different. At each company I have founded we had a strict rule. The receptionist was never a start-up position. The person who answered the phone had to have at least six months of experience, working in different departments, before he or she was allowed to take the prestige job of receptionist.

When people called our company, they got someone who was friendly, dynamic and knowledgeable.

Recently, I called a company and asked for Fred Jones. The receptionist said, in a dull voice, "What department does he work in?" I said, "He is the president of the company." "Oh," said the receptionist in a bored, nasal twang. "I guess that would be administration. That would be extension 216."

What kind of phone call do your customers get when they call your company? Is the person answering your phone energetic, with a clear, happy and enthusiastic voice?

We always had a mirror in front of everyone who was on the telephone, whether it was a customer service person or a receptionist. We asked them to look in the mirror while they talked—and to smile. That's right, smile. Even though the customer can't see you, you will sound different when you are smiling. You will be peppy, happy and enthusiastic.

> - A *Savage Company* treats salespeople like heroes.
> - They are the foot soldiers, the fountain of income.

I worked with one company as a consultant and spent a few days riding around with the salespeople. I asked them what they liked and did not like about the company. Do you know their biggest grievance was? Christmas baskets! Yes, Christmas baskets.

I dug into this a little deeper. What was the problem?

Well, everyone in the company got a great big Christmas basket full of goodies. All the salespeople got a Christmas basket half the size, with half as many treats. I was stunned.

I talked to the CEO of the company and told him the story. He said, "Yes, that's right. The salespeople make more money than the in house employees, so they don't need as much. We wanted our employees to have a nice gift at Christmas to help make up for their lower salaries."

The guy said this with a straight face!

I wanted to scream at him, but kept my cool. I said, "You know, Charles, I understand how you feel, but look at it from the salesperson's perspective. They are out there every day, banging on doors, getting rejection, trying to keep a positive attitude and bringing in sales. We need to make them feel like part of the same team. I am getting a lot of feedback that there are two groups out there. The inside group and the outside group. The employees on the inside feel tension with the salespeople on the outside. You can fix that, Charles, and one of the easiest ways to do that would be to make sure they all get the same size Christmas basket. What do you think?"

Charles cleared his throat, muttered a bit, and reluctantly agreed. It was the beginning of a long process of corporate culture change. Starting with Christmas baskets, we gradually got the company working together as a team.

My biggest challenge was to change the mentality of the CEO. He was an engineer and did not like salespeople. I convinced him to go out and make sales calls with the salespeople and his attitude began to change.

We had a company picnic where everyone got together for the first time. They had tons of fun playing games and eating. We designed the place cards at the picnic tables so that "inside" families had to sit with "outside" families. By the end of the day, the outsiders were starting to feel like insiders.

Salespeople unable to make decisions

I worked with a chicken company. The salespeople called on grocery stores, from the simplest Mom and Pop rural country store to the most sophisticated chain of supermarkets. As usual, I started my consulting assignment by "getting in the trenches." I spent a few days with the salespeople calling on the customers. I wanted to see how the salespeople did their jobs, and how the customers reacted to the products.

The salespeople were fine. They worked hard, had a fine rapport with the customers and kept excellent records. But there was one fatal flaw that came up over and over. The salespeople had no power to make decisions. The biggest objection that the stores had was the hassle it took to make returns of unsold chicken. If chicken did not sell within a few days, they were able to return it, but they had to go through a grand inquisition to do it.

I asked the salespeople who made the decision to accept returns on chicken. "The management folks back at headquarters."

"How long does it take them?"

"Two or three days."

"Why does it take so long?"

"Because they are swamped with so many requests for credits."

"Would you like to be able to make those decisions yourself?"

"Absolutely!"

"How long would it take you?"

"Two seconds."

"Does your manager ever deny a request for a return?"

"No. After asking a bunch of questions, which irritate the customers, they eventually accept the return and give them credit."

"Then why do they bother taking all that time?"

"It's been their procedure for 30 years."

Later, I talked to the CEO of the chicken company and asked him why this rule was in place. "We have to make sure the customers don't take advantage of us."

"Bruce, why don't you let the salespeople make the decision?"

"They would always decide in favor of the customer."

"But I understand your management people always eventually decide in favor of the customer anyway—but only after annoying the hell out of all your customers."

"Really?"

"Really."

It took some persuading, but we finally persuaded Bruce to give the decision-making power to the salespeople. Sales rose 12% within the next 12 months, because the customers perceived the company to be friendly and easy.

The driver—the person who can ruin or assure your sale

There was one other problem with the chicken company: the delivery drivers. They were grouchy, sloppy and rude. The customers told me that they dreaded dealing with this chicken company because of the bureaucracy and the drivers.

Thus, we had a sales force that was earnest and hard working but was hampered by two elements of the company that they could not control. Once I persuaded Bruce to give decision-making power to the salespeople, I began to talk to him about the drivers. "Bruce, your drivers are killing you out there. I have seen them in action and I have talked with your customers. Your drivers are part of the sales team, but they don't think that way. They think of themselves as lowly drivers. They are treated as low-life peons. No one ever motivates, teaches, coaches, encourages or thanks them. I believe that 80% of your drivers can be taught to be terrific members of the sales team. You'll probably have to fire about 20% of them."

Again, Bruce was reluctant. Part of my plan was to give the drivers bonuses for excellent work. I wanted to elevate them in prestige and self-image. He was skeptical. He hated to spend money. However, we finally convinced him. We bought five new uniforms for each driver, so each driver could have a fresh clean uniform every day. We trained them how to smile and greet the customer, and how to thank them for their business. We installed a bonus plan whereby the drivers got a commission for extra sales made on the spot at time of delivery.

The salespeople were thrilled. The customers began to give positive feedback. My analysis had been mostly right. However, I was wrong on one thing. I had told Bruce he would have to fire about 20% of the drivers. 95% of the drivers responded enthusiastically to the new program and only 5% were fired.

Two obstacles were removed. The management bureaucracy was eliminated. The driver image and training were transformed. Sales and profitability increased dramatically.

Savage Sales Secret #7

Make each salesperson feel incredibly important

Praise instead of punishment

Traditional sales managers punish salespeople when they don't perform well. *Savage Sales Managers praise their salespeople* all the time, and bring out the best in them.

Spencer Hays is one of the greatest motivators I have ever known. He ran another division of the Southwestern Company while I worked with Ted Welch. In 1968, he formed a men's clothing company, called Tom James Company. After students had worked a few summers selling books and graduated from college, many of them went to work for Tom James.

I worked for Tom James for a few months before starting my first *savage* business. Working with Spencer was an exhilarating experience. I have never received *so much praise in so little time*. Every time he called me, he would start the conversation, "Is this that outstanding, amazing, incredible, unbelievable Steve Savage?" He said something similar to everyone, so it always made you chuckle, but by golly, it made you feel good!

If I had a good week, Spencer was lavish in his praise. *If I had a bad week, Spencer was equally generous in his commendations.* He would go into raptures over my character. "Steve, you are one of the most outstanding men I have ever known. You are the kind of guy I admire profoundly, because you never let a bad day or a bad week get you down. I'm not the least bit worried about your sales this week. That's just the law of averages working. You've swung that bat and had a few strikes. That means you're about to get a few hits and even a home run.

You have the courage and tenacity to stay with it. I believe in you. Have a wonderful week. And remember to say every morning:

> * *I feel healthy!*
> * *I feel happy!*
> * *I feel terrific!"*

He would repeat that kind of tribute to all his salespeople all the time and we all felt wonderful. We wanted to work to make Spencer proud of us.

Recently, 40 years later, I talked with Spencer on the phone. I knew it was Spencer because the phone call started out: *"Is this that outstanding, amazing, incredible, unbelievable Steve Savage?"* Yes, it sounds corny, and I had to laugh, but by golly, *after all these years, it still felt good!*

Spencer's philosophy has made the Tom James Company a special place for a salesperson to work. The sales managers are not called "managers." They are called *"leaders."* They *lead* people. They lead by example and by motivation.

Each leader at Tom James has his or her own customers. Thus, when you ask your salespeople to go out and make sales calls, you are not asking them to do something that you aren't doing yourself—every single day.

When a Tom James leader looks for salespeople, he or she does not necessarily look for a person with a sales background. They look for a person with a strong work ethic. Did this person face a difficult choice in life? At that point, did she make the right choice, work harder and stick with it? Does this person have above-average character and integrity? Is he teachable?

If the answers to those questions are "yes," the person is hired. The testimony to the Tom James philosophy is the raw number: at the end of the first year: 83% of the new hires are still with the company. Very few companies have that high a retention rate.

What is the secret?

Yes, everyone feels incredibly important. Yes, they are told how great they are. Yes, the leaders use the Spencer Hays messages like "I feel healthy, I feel happy, and I feel terrific."

> • However, the *fundamentals of the pay structure, bonuses and stock incentives are just as important.*

The new person gets a reasonable base, which is not considered a salary, but a commission. It is guaranteed during the first few months. Thus, while a person is getting started, he or she can relax and learn the job. This is a great way to start getting *high productivity without high pressure.*

The training is hands-on. No theory or ivory-tower. The leader takes the trainee out on her sales calls. The leader also joins the trainee on his sales calls. In the next chapter, we will talk about the "soft" approach, the "soft" presentation" and the "soft" close. But at this point, we want to emphasize the fundamental fact that each person feels incredibly important.

The results are astonishing. The average first year person earns $60,000. The top salesperson earns over $100,000 his first year.

But that is not all. *Each salesperson is given options to buy company stock.* The options are granted at the end of the very first year. The option is exercised after ten years. Now, that is a way to keep a person with the company!

When the option time comes, if the person does not have the cash to exercise her option, she can deduct it from the increased value of the stock. Let's say the stock option was worth $5,000. Ten years later the stock is worth $50,000. The person does not have $5,000 in cash. That's OK. Instead of getting $50,000 in actual stock, she gets $45,000 worth of actual stock.

Furthermore, during the 10 years the salesperson is paid dividends each year on that stock, as though he already owned the stock. Talk about feeling incredibly important! Why would anyone ever want to leave?

Experienced salespeople earn $250,000 to $350,000 a year. Some experienced people have earned as much as $1,000,000 a year. This includes personal sales as well as the *sales leadership dividend*.

- Note: they do not talk about a management commission. They talk about a *"sales leadership dividend."*
- Again, each salesperson feels *incredibly important*—and it is not just words. *It is money.*

Savage Sales Secret #8

Make each customer feel incredibly important

Spencer Hays knew how to make his salespeople feel incredibly important. He also taught us how to make our customers feel extraordinarily important. He founded Tom James Company to give an opportunity to the young men who had been through a few summers selling books door-to-door with Southwestern.

Spencer loved fine clothes, but he hated to go shopping. He figured other executives felt the same way. So, he designed a marketing system to cater specifically to the busy executive.

The salesperson would call on the executive, show him the latest fine fabrics and fashionable styles, take his order and take his deposit. The customer had to make only one visit to our store—to have his picture taken by our sophisticated camera that took his picture from several different angles, and to have his measurements taken by our tailor. After that, he never had to come to our store again.

Spencer taught us to use the same greeting on the phone that he always used with us. When we called a CEO of a company, the phone call always started out, "Is this that outstanding, successful, amazing Andrew Jones?" We said it *slowly*, with sincerity.

Usually the guy would laugh and say, "You gotta be kidding. Who is this anyway?"

The ice was broken. All I had to say was, "I'm Steve Savage, with Tom James Company. You know Bill Lee? *I'm his tailor.* He just bought a couple of suits from me and thought you would look terrific with one of our custom-tailored suits. Bill said you're extremely busy but you're a great dresser. He liked me because I came to him and he didn't have to bother going shopping. I'm going to be in your area Thursday afternoon and I was wondering if I could stop by so you could take a quick look at some of our new fabrics. It will take only a couple of minutes. I'm available at either 2:30 or 3:45. Would either of those times be convenient for you?"

(I always had to resist my natural instinct to speak fast. Spencer taught us how to say all the above *slowly*.)

The sales pitch was powerful but low-key. We kept it friendly and humorous. Our only objective at this point was to get an appointment to show him the fabrics.

This is the "soft" way to get an appointment over the phone. Notice that I introduced myself as the person's *tailor*. In my appraisal business, I introduced myself as the *appraiser*. It is always useful to think of a phrase to call yourself that sets yourself up as a professional that will give the customer something of value—not just a sales pitch.

You can use a similar "soft" approach when you are making a cold call. Usually we made our appointments on the phone, but if we had a cancellation, and had a few free minutes, we would stop by an office and say to the receptionist. "Hi, I'm Steve Savage. I am Bill Lee's tailor. I was just over in his office. He thought that Jim Jackson would like to know about me. May I see him for just a minute?" Once again, a "soft" approach is non-threatening and often gets you in the door.

Once we showed him the fabrics and the styles, he was usually sold. He liked the convenience of being able to order right there in his office. Our suits were expensive, but we were not competing on price. We were competing on super service. These executives were willing to pay more for incredible service.

> - We made them feel important and they bought from us.
> - They became loyal customers and would not think of going anywhere else.

After a few years, Spencer got feedback from the salespeople that there was only *one major flaw* in the system. The executive had to make that one lousy trip to the store to get his picture and measurements taken. Some executives never showed up. Others kept postponing. It was an inconvenience. Spencer wanted to make it *easy for the customer to do business* with Tom James.

Thus, a major decision was made. Rip out the cameras. A huge investment in expensive cameras was thrown into the garbage. Many corporations get way too hung up on their investment in equipment and forget about the customer. But not Spencer Hays! The customer came first. He had to make the *customer feel incredibly important.*

From that point onward, the salesperson had to acquire a new skill. He had to be able to measure the customer—and to do it right. (Notice that I am still saying *"he"* had to do it. Tom James still had all-male sales force back in the early 70's.)

Bill Yonke has been with Tom James for 17 years. Recently, he told me how times have changed since I worked with the company back in 1970. Now, the salesperson goes to the executive's office, shows him the fabrics and styles, whips out his measuring tape, writes up the order, gets the deposit and leaves. Six weeks later, the suit arrives. The executive is thrilled. He never has to leave his office.

Today there are 125 Tom James stores in the United States, Australia, and Europe. There are over 480 salespeople. There are four cloth manufacturers in various countries and three plants with trained tailors that assemble the suits per specifications for each individual customer.

Each store has a telemarketing unit where the salespeople gather each afternoon to make phone calls, supervised by a sales manager who also makes his or her own sales. About 65% of the sales force is composed of men with 35% women. However, 60% of the new hires are women. The corporate culture has changed since the days back in the early 70's when I was one of the "guys" selling suits!

The key to making the customer feel incredibly important:

1. Initial phone call showing humor, respect and friendliness
2. Easy and gentle way of setting up an appointment
3. Low-keyed manner of presenting the product
4. Making it incredibly easy to buy

Break the ice

Most salespeople tend to do way too much talking. At Tom James, Bill Yonke is a sales leader. He lets the customer do at least 50% of the talking. This makes the customer feel incredibly important. Also, you don't bore him to death with a sales pitch. Further, you automatically convert your "pitch" into a "soft" presentation that easily glides to a "soft" close. Here are some of the questions Bill asks, many of which you can ask no matter what business you are in:

- What do you do here?
- Have you heard of us?
- What have you heard?
- Where do you usually shop when you buy a suit?
- What's important to you?
- In order to win your business, what would you expect from me?
- What would I have to do to get and keep your business?
- Do you like to shop?
- Do you have time to shop?
- Do you usually get advice from the salespeople when you buy a suit?

You need to have a few key points that define your company in your customer's mind. With Tom James, there are five key ingredients:

- Convenience
- Selection
- Service
- Style
- Fit

As Bill gently asks these questions, he tries to figure out which of those five features is the "hot button" of the customer and focuses on that issue.

If the person was into "style," he will often say something like, "Often you go to a store and you find 90% of what you're looking for, but you have to settle for that last 10%. With us you can get 100% of what you want."

A good presentation closes itself

If you have asked a lot of questions, and found the customer's "hot button," you can do a "soft" close without any pressure. You have made the customer feel incredibly important. At Tom James, Bill will usually say something simple like, "OK. Stand up. Let me take your measurements." That's it. The sale is done. A classic "soft" close.

> • Another way to *gently close the sale in a "soft" way is to talk about the date you will deliver the product.*

"Let's see, today is the 27th of June. We are scheduling deliveries for the first part of August. If I schedule yours for the first week of August, would that be OK?"

Another classic "soft" close. The answer is almost always "yes."

The corporate vision

Your corporate vision needs to communicate itself to your employees, your salespeople and your customers. The Tom James' corporate vision conveys in a few short words exactly what the company is all about: "*We Come To You with Fine Clothing.*" These seven words let the customer and the salespeople know precisely what the company means and stands for.

From "me" to "you"

I worked as a consultant for a supermarket chain in Central America. To start my assignment, I visited all the supermarkets in the chain in three cities. Then I visited all the competitors.

They were all fairly similar. Some had slightly better displays. Some were better lighted. Some had wider aisles. In general, my client's stores were on a par with the competition. What could we do that would make us different?

We got together for a brainstorming session. I asked the CEO to bring an assortment of employees, from store managers to check-out clerks. We had a group of 20 people sitting in the conference room.

They all knew me because I had visited their stores. The CEO laughingly referred to me as the "Savage Guerrilla." (*El Guerrillero Salvaje.*) The clerks especially liked me because I remembered their names and complimented them on their work.

I asked them, "What do you think that we do better than any other supermarket in Nicaragua?"

We got different answers, but the consensus seemed to be that we treated our customers better than anyone else. I was not convinced, because I had seen the other supermarkets in action, and felt they were all about the same, but I did not say anything yet.

Then I asked, "OK, you've been to my *Savage Marketing* seminar. Remember, one of our themes was that a *Savage Company* (*Una Empresa Salvaje*) could do things that were either free or cost very little money. What can you think we could do that would be free or cost almost nothing?"

We got several good ideas, but then one of the clerks suggested, *"What if we offered a free shoe shine to every customer?"*

Pow!

What an idea! The only cost would be a shoe-shine boy, and that was minimal. Everyone loved the idea—and I bragged about Alicia, the clerk, who had come up with the best idea of all. She grinned from ear to ear.

Two days later they started *shining shoes, free, for every customer.*

Within six months, the supermarket's sales had increased 9%. Within a year, sales had increased 12%. And the only change was the free shoeshine.

> • The key was thinking about *"you" the customer* instead of "me" the company.

Savage Sales Secret #9

Raise your sales through brilliant telemarketing

Earlier, I told you the story of Mike and radiators. He grew his company by making it easy for his customers. After the company was sold, the new owners asked me to help them as a consultant. My mission: to set up a telemarketing operation.

The company, under Mike's leadership, had solved the problem of quick deliveries to customers in metropolitan areas. The new owners quickly set about setting up warehouses in all the major cities in the USA. However, there were vast areas of the country where it was not practical to set up a warehouse. In the rural areas, the only solution was to ship a radiator to the customer by UPS or FedEx. This was still fantastic service, because the mechanic could get the radiator overnight—much faster than he could get it anywhere else.

My job was to set up a telemarketing operation to contact every single mechanic, body shop and car dealer in the rural areas of the USA.

Now, how do you get the attention of a mechanic who is lying under a car, covered with grease?

The key is to make your telemarketing call low-keyed, business like and different from your standard telemarketing pitch. And you need to offer something free to get their attention. And it has to be short. So, here's how it goes:

"Hi, is this Joe? This is Rita from 1-800-Radiator. I have a $25 coupon to send you for your next radiator and just wanted to check real quickly to make sure I have your correct address. Are you at 123 Main Street? Great! Is your zip code 99364? Perfect! I'll get that coupon in the mail today.

(You got his attention! You have him relaxed. You now have permission to go on.)

"By the way, we have over 1,800 different part numbers in stock. We can get you just about any radiator for any car or truck built in the past 30 years. Have you heard about us? Where do you usually get your radiators? If you call us, we can guarantee overnight service. And we have a lifetime warranty on each radiator. Do you have any radiator jobs you'd like me to give you a quote on?"

That's it. Sometimes the mechanic had a car in the shop and gave us the specifications on the phone. We'd give him a quote and usually made a sale. If not, he got the coupon in the mail a few days later.

Within two years, we had gained 3,471 new customers for the company resulting in over $2,000,000 in business per year. It was all incremental business. Without a dynamic telemarketing program, it never would have happened.

The keys to our telemarketing efforts were:

1. Offer something free
2. Make it businesslike
3. Have a script
4. Don't talk in a sing-song voice
5. Have a "soft" close. "May I give you a quote?" is a lot better than "Would you like to buy?"

Telemarketing in Mexico

My friend Tomás asked me to invest with him in a new company called *Apoyo Escolar* (School Support). It had a similar concept to the fund raising company we had formed in Mexico back in 1991, back when we were a division of IFS/Colgate Palmolive. Since then, the company had gone through a couple of changes of ownership. There were difficulties with the program with the Secretary of Education (which I have described in vivid detail in my book ***Guerrilla Business Secrets***). Eventually, the USA company lost interest in the Mexican subsidiary and shut it down.

Tomás was convinced that the idea had merit and that we could help the 100,000 schools in Mexico raise the money they needed for computers, equipment and other school needs. He felt that he could establish a genuine Mexican company that would address the uncertainties that had been raised by some of the offices of the Secretary of Education. Their main concerns were:

1. The profits were going from Mexico to the USA
2. The products were made in China
3. The students were losing classroom time

On point #1, there was a great deal of misunderstanding. Yes, a small amount of profit went to the parent company in the USA. But the Mexican company made the bulk of the profit. Most people understood this. However, some bureaucrats, like government bureaucrats in every country (including the USA), did not understand economics very well and continued to set up obstacles.

Tomás addressed these three issues boldly and intelligently. He made sure that all the company literature stated the following:

1. This was a Mexican company and all money stayed in Mexico
2. All products were made in Mexico
3. All sales were done by parents

In addition, Tomás decided to reduce the costs of the operation by using a telemarketing sales force instead of a field sales force. Back in the IFS days, we had 80 salespeople covering Mexico. Now, with a group of eight telemarketers, we could cover the same schools efficiently and at a much lower cost.

On our first call to the school, we usually contact either the principal (called the "director") or the PTA president. Just like in the radiator phone call, we don't try to sell anything on the first phone call. This is a business-to-business phone call. We want everyone to be relaxed and create some interest.

The phone call goes like this:

"Hi, Mr. Director. This is Martha, from Apoyo Escolar. We help schools raise money for special needs such as computers and other equipment. We helped Morales School raise $10,300 pesos in one week. They bought three computers. Do you know Maestro Jaime over there?

"I want to send you an information package so you can learn more about how we can help you raise money. I just wanted to check your address. Are you at XXX Street? Is xxxxx your correct postal code? OK! Great! I'll send it to you right away.

"Also, a lot of school directors ask me to send an information package to the PTA president. Who is in charge of your PTA? Great! Shall I send a package for her also? Would it be easier if I sent it to her home instead of the school? Do you happen to have her phone number?

"If I could help you raise $10,000 pesos, what would be your most urgent need right now?"

Do you see the relationship between the two phone calls? It does not matter if you are selling radiators or fund raising programs. It does not matter if you are in the USA or Mexico. The principles are the same.

1. Offer something free—in this case, an information package
2. Make it businesslike
3. Have a script
4. Don't talk in a sing-song voice
5. Have a "soft" close. ""If I could help you raise $10,000 pesos, what would be your most urgent need right now?" is a lot better than, "Would you like to do a fund raising program?"

How to avoid "voice jail."

How many times have you found yourself talking to someone's voice mail? My friend Rory Vaden calls it *"voice jail!"*

First, you can often avoid getting into voice jail by properly talking with the secretary or assistant. Her instinct and training drive her to get rid of you and into her boss' voice mail as soon as possible. You can make her feel comfortable and relaxed with you by being relaxed yourself. If you set up a conflict, she will win. So, relax, go easy and you will get what you want. What do you want? You want to talk directly to the boss. You do not want to leave a message. You do not want to go to voice jail. So here is a routine that will help you relax and get the job done:

"ABC Company. May I help you?"

"Yes. I'm Steve Savage. (Slowly) I'm calling Suzanne Jones."

"Let me put you through to her secretary."

"Suzanne Jones' office, Mary speaking."

"Hi Mary! I'm Steve Savage. I'm calling Suzanne Jones."

"What company are you with?"

"Savage International. Just tell her that Betty Harkins asked me to call her."

"Ms. Jones is in a meeting. I'll have her call you. What is your number?"

"OK! Great. What time will her meeting be over?"

"About 11:00."

"Perfect. I'll call her at 11:05."

Then you hang up. You agreed with everything she said, but you stayed in control. You did not give her your number. Why? Because it is a waste of time. Suzanne Jones will not call you back. You will be frustrated. But you didn't get into a fight with Mary the secretary. You agreed with everything she said and you remained friendly. In the end, you got what you wanted—a good time to call her back. The next time you call, Mary the secretary will be a little friendlier because she remembers you from last time.

So, now let's say you call back and Mary suggests voice mail. Here's how it goes:

"Hey Mary! Steve Savage calling back. Is Suzanne out of that meeting?"

"No, they are still going hot and heavy. Let me put you through to her voice mail."

"Let's do this. I know Suzanne and you are really busy. I have to go to a meeting myself. What time this afternoon would be the best time to call her back?"

"Well, I guess she'll be available at about 3:00 PM."

"Perfect! I'll call you at 3:00! Thanks so much for your help!"

Again, *you avoided leaving a message and you avoided voice jail.* You remained friendly with Mary and you found out a good time to call back. The third time you call back, Mary is much more likely to put you through. She is the one who told you the time to call back. You treated her with respect and friendliness. And you get what you want— and phone connection with the boss!

How to find the decision maker

When you first call a company, you may not know with whom to speak, unless you have gotten a specific lead from someone else (which is ideal—but you don't always have the ideal situation)!

Guard dogs

Receptionists, secretaries and assistants are trained to be guard dogs. Their job is to protect their boss from interruptions. Your job is to make sure the boss has a clear vision of how your product or service can make the boss a hero and make the company prosper. You can accomplish your mission if you work skillfully and tactfully with the guard dogs. Think of a puppy you have trained. You made that little dog lovable and cooperative. Now think of Stella Rasmussen, the guard dog, with her arms crossed, her forehead wrinkled and her eyes glowering. Your job is to make Stella lovable and cooperative just like you did your little puppy.

Stella has learned all the tricks to get rid of you. You will be successful if you have fun and view this as a merry game. You are going to make Stella your friend and you are going to talk with the decision maker in this company. Your attitude needs to positive, calm and relaxed.

Here are a few techniques you can use to turn that vicious guard dog into a sweet little puppy.

"Sorry, he's out of the office."

"OK. No problem. Could we page him?"

Often this works. Stella the guard dog is not used to this, so you caught her off guard. You didn't argue. You agreed with her. Then you just asked a simple question.

Let's suppose that does not work. OK. Go on to step two.

"OK. That's fine. Does he have a business cell? Great. Let's do this. How about if you call him on his cell phone and as soon as you reach him you can connect us."

Notice the magic phrase "let's do this." Stella and you are doing this together. You aren't ordering her around. You aren't arguing. You are working with her, politely and smoothly, to solve a problem. You are converting her from a snarling guard dog to a lovable puppy.

Let's suppose you are trying to reach a manager who does not have his or her own office, but works in an area with several other people. Stella tells you that the manager is on the phone.

You say, "OK. No problem. Can you transfer me to someone who sits next o her?"

Again, you have given Stella a solution she never thought of before. The surly guard dog becomes a tender puppy.

If you are not sure if you have the right person, here is a great question to ask, "OK. That's fine. Is there someone of equal business rank that I should talk to?" Remember, you want to get through to the decision-maker in the company, so this question might flush out exactly the right person for you.

Remember to keep great notes. Always write down the names of everybody with whom you speak, whether it is on the phone or in person. If you have spoken with several people on the phone, it is wonderful to have their names in your head when you go to the business for a visit. They immediately like you and the word spreads around that you are a person with whom they would like to do business.

If you write these notes on a piece of paper, make sure you transfer them to your computer the same day. Get them into whatever contact management program you are using, whether it is Outlook, ACT, Gold Mine or any other program. Get everyone's name and write down any comments that will help you when you call them back or visit them.

The higher the better

When you present your program to a company, the higher up you can go the better. If you can get in to see the CEO, (or talk to him or her on the phone) that is fantastic. You may not need to spend a lot of time with the CEO. But if the CEO likes you and your product, you will have a lot easier time of it as you talk with people at lower ranks.

Let's say that the person who will decide on your product is the plant manager. But before you talked with the plant manager, you talked with the CEO. You described your product and your program. Charlie, the CEO liked it. Then Charlie told you, "You know, this sounds pretty good. But Tom, our plant manager, is the guy that handles all this. Give him a call."

Then you say, "Great. I'll do that. Is Tom the one that makes the decisions on this? Does he have a budget for this?"

- If the answer is "yes," then Tom is your man.
- If the answer is "no," then you need to find out who actually makes the decisions.
- That is the person to whom you want to speak.

OK. Let's say that Charlie the CEO told you, "Yes, Tom has the budget and, yes, Tom makes the decisions." Now you have enormous power when you call Tom for the first time. Instead of calling Tom cold, out of the blue, your conversation will go like this:

"Hey Tom, I'm Steve Savage, with Global Plastics. Charlie Stiller and I were just talking about plastics and he asked me to give you a call. He told me you're the guy that makes all the decisions about this. I'm going to be in your area tomorrow and I was wondering if I could drop by for about twelve minutes to introduce myself and let you know what we have. Would 1:30 be convenient for you or would 3:00 be better?"

Talk about credibility! How can Tom say "no?" You made two phone calls, one to Charlie and one to Tom. But on the second call with Tom you have the power of Charlie's endorsement. You will walk in to see Tom with confidence and strength. You will make a sale.

Savage Sales Secret #10

Remember the opera AIDA

The radiator company gave me two missions. I told you about the first: setting up the telemarketing operation. My second mission was to set up a field sales force east of the Mississippi. The California company was pretty well established in the West, but was moving aggressively to become dominant coast-to-coast.

My goal was the same as it had been since I was a 19-year-old college kid selling books door-to-door: *get high productivity without high pressure.*

How do you convince the owner of an auto body shop or an auto repair shop to buy radiators from you instead of from good old Joe's Radiator Shop where he's been buying for the last 20 years? Here is how we did it: a *soft* approach, a *soft* presentation and a *soft* close.

Picture this: the mechanic is covered with grease, lying under a car. He doesn't want to talk with you. He has to get the car finished by 11 AM when the customer is going to pick up the car. You have to be quick.

I remembered the four steps that my friend Jay Levinson had taught me back in 1981 when we first started working together. Jay asked me, "Steve, do you remember the opera Aida?"

"Yes," I replied, "but how is that gonna help me?"

"Simple," said Jay. "Here's how it works:"

A = Attention

I = Interest

D = Desire

A = Action

Back in 1981, Jay helped me design direct mail pieces with the AIDA philosophy. I have used this simple but profound principle ever since, both in marketing materials and in sales talks.

In going into an auto repair shop, AIDA works like this:

A = Attention

"Hi, Joe! I'm Steve with 1-800-Radiator. Have you heard about me yet? OK! I just wanted to check with you real quick."

I = Interest

"I wanted to drop off this $25 coupon for your next radiator purchase. We have 1,800 different part numbers in stock and can have your radiator delivered within one hour. Does that sound pretty good?"

D = Desire

"We have a lifetime warranty on each radiator. We can get you just about any radiator on any car or truck built in the last 30 years."

A = Action

"Can I get you a quote on a radiator? I can call and get you a price real quick."

That was it. Low-keyed, friendly and businesslike. We had our salespeople make 50 visits per day. The business grew in quantum leaps.

- Apply the same AIDA steps to your sales process and your business will grow in quantum leaps as well.

Savage Sales Secret #11

Create a sales empire by focusing on what makes you special

From "my product" to "my client"

Kimberly-Clark has always had a large operation in Mexico. But in the past few years, their self-concept has changed. They used to think of themselves as a paper company. They produced great products made of paper.

Gradually, they began to realize that their real power was marketing and branding rather than production. I became aware of the power of their brand when I started to travel on business in Mexico in 1990, setting up a subsidiary for a division of Colgate Palmolive. (See my book *Guerrilla Business Secrets* for details on that great adventure!)

One day I went into a small store in Oaxaca, a charming town in southern Mexico. I was sniffling and needed a pack of tissues. I described what I needed to the sales clerk, in Spanish: "I need a soft paper tissue, because I have a cold, I am sniffling and I need to blow my nose." "Oh, sí, Señor," she replied, helpfully. The word for that in Spanish is "Kleenex!"

I laughed and bought a pack of Kleenex. But then I pondered the power of their brand. The word "Kleenex" had truly become synonymous with "tissue" in Spanish just as it has in English.

Kimberly Clark made a conscious decision to focus their energy and attention on their ability to brand a product and market it—and to let their skill in production and paper-making follow. Thus, they no longer think of themselves as a production company or as a paper company. *They think of themselves as a marketing company that has a fantastic ability to come up with great brands and to market them.*

Think of these brands: Viva, Scott, Cottonelle, Snuggies, Wypall, Fiesta, KleenGuard, Kotex, Depend, DryNites and Huggies, among others. You will recognize products within the health and hygiene field that have developed powerful brands that are part of your visual scan every time you go shopping. They are all Kimberly Clark brands.

- What is your strength?
- What makes your company special?
- What makes your creative juices flow?
- What gets you excited?
- Most of all, what value do you bring to your customer?

Savage Sales Secret #12

Eliminate rules

Transform your company from a bulky elephant to a wily cockroach

Elephants have survived for 25,000 years. Cockroaches have survived for 25,000,000 years.

What kind of company do you have? Is your company a bulky *elephant*, a *bloated bureaucracy* that has trouble moving from A to B without endless discussions and constant worrying about rules? Or is your company a *cockroach*, which *goes over, under, around and through all obstacles*?

- Most companies have too many rules.
- Think about your rules.
- How many are really necessary?
- Which rules slow you down?
- Is there a rule that causes you to annoy a customer and lose a sale?
- Do you have rules that tie your salespeople up in knots?

You can transform your company from bored employees to *motivated Savages* by eliminating rules and giving your people the power to make decision. Here is a great example:

I worked as a consultant for a company that had a chain of 220 appliance stores. Their sales were flat and they asked me to help them figure out how to rev up sales and get profitability restored. As always in any consulting assignment, my first job was to "hit the trenches." I visited one store in a poor neighborhood. It was very large and well-lighted—but with almost no customers.

I asked Ralph, the store manager, what was happening. Ralph shook his head and confided in me. "Three years ago, the company made a rule that our minimum store size had to be 4,000 square feet. We had a little 1,500 square-foot store that was making money. It was a family-style store, perfect for this community. We had to close it to conform to the new rules. Now we're losing money."

The brilliant people that made the rule were 2,000 miles away. I reported back to them what I had seen. They asked me what I recommended. I said, "Trust Ralph. He understands his store and his market. Whatever you do, don't give him a rule. Let him make his own rules."

They were skeptical, but they had paid me a lot of money, so they reluctantly agreed.

Ralph selected a new site, downsized the store, cut the rent in half and converted it into a family-type operation appropriate to the neighborhood.

> - One rule eliminated.
> - One manager elevated.
> - Profitability returned.

Analyze your company. Tomorrow, get with your colleagues and *figure out at least one rule you can eliminate.*

Savage Sales Secret #13

Give power to your salespeople without losing control

You will demolish your competition when you make your salespeople "owners" of their territories and their customers.

Analyze your company. Are your salespeople able to make decisions, on-the-spot, face-to-face with a customer? Or do they have to go through a painful approval process that keeps the customer hanging in limbo?

Ceramics sale lost

I worked as a consultant with a ceramics company. As usual, my favorite part was spending time "*in the trenches*" with the salespeople. I rode around with Adam and listened to his story of woe. He had sold $100,000 worth of tile to an architect who was designing an apartment building. The tile was for all the bathrooms. But the architect wanted a discount. "Look! I'm giving you $100,000 worth of business. I want a 10% discount."

Adam had no power. So he trudged back to his store manager. She had a little bit of power. She could go up to 3%. Adam called the architect and with great enthusiasm, declared, "I can get you a 3% discount!"

"3%!" snarled the architect. "I'm giving you $100,000 worth of business. Give me 10% or forget it."

Adam had to call Gunther, the Vice President of Finance at company headquarters, 1,000 miles away. Gunther hated discounts. But he hated to lose a sale. So after several more days of pondering the issue, he finally approved the 10% discount.

Adam called the architect with great excitement. "I've got good news! I've got you your 10%!"

What do you think happened?

You know the result.

The architect had bought the tile from someone else—from a *Savage Salesperson* who could make a decision on the spot, in the field, face-to-face with the customer.

What is it like in your company? What kind of commission structure do you have? Have you designed your salary and bonus configuration so the salesperson can make intelligent decisions that are profitable for the company and still attractive to the customer?

Design your commission arrangement so the salesperson participates in the profitability of the company. Then he or she will make intelligent decisions, knowing that their commissions and bonuses will be based on the profit they generated for the company.

> - *The customer wins*
> - *The salesperson wins*
> - *The company wins.*

Appliance sale lost

I worked as a consultant for a company that had a chain of 220 appliance stores. One day I was observing the salespeople in one store, watching the way they handled their customers. A young couple walked in, excited, newly married, with $2,500 to spend on appliances. Their grandmother had given them a gift certificate for their wedding present.

With great enthusiasm, they picked out a stove, washer and dryer, refrigerator and TV set. The total came to $2,700. The couple asked for a $200 discount, since all they had was a $2,500 gift certificate. The salesperson had no power. The store manager had no power. They called the regional sales manager. He had no power. They called the marketing director. He had power but he was in a meeting. And of course, a meeting is a lot more important than a customer!

The young couple walked out, went to another appliance store and got what they wanted for $2,500. I was horrified. When I talked to the General Manager of the chain of stores, I related the story and asked him why the salesperson or the store manager could not have made the decision, immediately, to give them a discount. Why did they have to go through the marketing director, who was not available?

"Well, the marketing director has all the analysis of costs in his computer," was the lame reply.

I felt like screaming. The store manager had a computer. Why couldn't she look at the same numbers? We analyzed the situation and *changed the rules.* After that the company gave power to the salespeople, but also designed the commission structure so that their bonuses were affected by the profitability they gave to the company. Thus, *salespeople could make on-the-spot decisions.* Salespeople now had power. They would prefer to make a lower commission than to lose a sale.

> * *The company won.*
> * *The salesperson won.*
> * *The customer won.*

Savage Sales Secret #14

Think how the typical salesperson does it, then do the opposite

Contrarian sales secrets

The *Savage Salesperson* is a contrarian. You do things differently than the typical Salesperson.

- The typical Salesperson does 95% of the talking, yak yak yak. The *Savage Salesperson* asks a lot of questions, sits back and listens, and makes sure the customer does at <u>least</u> 50% of the talking.

- The typical Salesperson talks in a sing-song voice, so we talk in a natural voice.

- The typical Salesperson dresses in an uncomfortable suit and tie, so we dress casually.

- The typical Salesperson carries a briefcase so we just carry a notebook or a clipboard.

- The typical Salesperson gives a high pressure pitch so we give it real low-key, personal and professional.

- The typical salesperson hangs around too long and annoys people so we are always in a hurry, dashing in and out of the customer's business or home quickly.

Savage Sales Secret #15

Sell through intelligent preparation and performance

Mimi is the best real estate salesperson I have ever known. She was a good friend of ours, but we had never done business with her. However, I had often heard of her real estate excellence through mutual friends. When we decided to move, she was our obvious choice.

We asked her to do two things at once:

1. Sell our current home
2. Find us our dream home—with at least five acres, a horse barn and a riding arena.

Mimi knew exactly what to do. She quickly got us to repaint a few rooms and get our house ready to sell.

We have bought and sold many homes over the years. Usually it is a nightmare, with the real estate person parading an endless troop of curiosity seekers through your house, disturbing your tranquility and upsetting your life.

Mimi brought only three people to our home. They were all hot prospects. My wife and I never saw any of them because she arranged for them to come when we were out. Within one week, we had a purchase and sale agreement.

She did not waste our time, the customer's time or her time. She figured out what the prospects wanted, what they could afford and then she showed them the house that fit their needs. She did not have to use high pressure. She simply used intelligent matching of prospect with property.

The same thing happened when she showed us our dream property. She showed us only three properties. She knew which one we were going to pick, but she showed us two others just so we would be satisfied that we had looked around at various possibilities. She knew what we wanted and needed. She asked all the right questions, knew what kind of place we wanted and how much we were willing to invest. She was intelligent and efficient. Although she is one of the most charming and delightful people we have ever known, she did not sell based on her charm. She sold based on intelligent planning and matching of people and property.

Recently I talked with Mimi about her philosophy of selling real estate. Let me share with you some *Mimi wisdom*:

"Well, Steve, it really boils down to hard work. You have to work hard to make it happen. It won't fall in your lap.

"You have to remember the primary thing. You're not really a salesperson. You are a *counselor*. Your job is to counsel people. You need to find out what they need and want. Your objective has to be to be of service to your client.

"You have to be an *organizer*. You put everything together to make it work. Once it gets into escrow, everything starts. It can unravel if you don't keep your eyes on every detail. You have to be a watch dog. Your job is to make sure it comes out right. You can't relax until escrow closes.

"It's a service type of business. A realtor has two things to deal with: 1) the seller and 2) the buyer.

How to work with the seller

"With the seller, you need to learn everything you can about the property. I specialize in horse properties, so I go out and walk the land. I want the most recent survey and I want to know the property lines. I find the corners. If there is not a survey, I use the USGS (United States Geological Survey) maps.

"With a residential property, it is smaller and easier. You still want to know where the corners are. Sometimes the owner knows, but you can't count on it. Sometimes you need to recommend a survey. Just tell the owner, 'You know, it's in your best interest to have a survey.'"

"You need a plat map. When you sell, you need to know the properties around the property you are selling. You need to know the zoning. You need a preliminary title report, with restrictions and easements. Be aware of the CC and R—Covenants, Conditions and Restrictions.

"I also ask a lot of point-blank questions like, 'Do you have noisy neighbors?' You need to tell the potential buyer if there are any problems. If you are thorough it helps both you and the seller. It keeps us both out of trouble!

"You need to find out the seller's time frame. Ask questions like, 'Is there a major reason why you have to do things quickly?'

"Don't take every listing. If they are asking too much, it's not worth my trouble. I have to believe in the property and the price is part of my belief."

"When everything is in escrow, I want to be sure everything goes smoothly. I never count on it until escrow closes. I take backup offers. I will put "pending" on the "for sale" sign. I don't put "sold" until escrow has closed.

Do you have any doubts as to why Mimi is so successful?

How to work with the buyer

Mimi then told me how she works with the buyer. She is just as thorough as she was with the Seller.

"I want to know what the buyer's hopes and dreams are. I am a consultant. I ask about their lifestyle. I want to know if this will be their permanent home and whether they consider this to be a long-term investment.

"I ask them for their financial information and ask for permission to talk with their banker. I don't want to waste time showing them homes that are too expensive, that they can't afford. I will ask the banker to tell me whether the buyer can afford the price range he or she is talking to me about. I want to hear the banker say to me, 'Yes, this person is a candidate for this price range.' This completely eliminates taking people who are not qualified."

"Also, the banker might let me know that the person can afford a more expensive property. In that case, I have a little more freedom. I might show them properties in a higher range. But I don't push it. I only do it if I feel it fits their needs and desires."

How to promote a property

I asked Mimi how she promotes her properties, and what kind of money she spends on advertising.

"I list it with MLS immediately. That is the very first thing I do. I don't wait.

"Then I contact other brokers who specialize in that category of property. I know brokers who specialize in horse properties like I do. If I have a first-time home buyer, I know which brokers to call. If I have a commercial listing, I call my commercial broker friends. They may have clients waiting to buy precisely what I have just listed.

"As far as advertising, it all depends on the target. You need to target the people you think would be looking for this type of property. If it is a high end horse property, I will obviously advertise in the horse magazines. I will use the Wall Street Journal or other quality publications. If it is a first-time buyer, I may use the local newspaper.

"But it is amazing how much can be done through word of mouth. Make friends with everyone. Realtors can help each other. In the horse world, we can call around and find out who is looking for property and who is selling property."

Know your property

I knew Mimi was a specialist in horse properties. I asked her what she did if she got a listing for something unusual and different.

"Let's say you get a listing for a vineyard. If you don't know anything about vineyards, find out. Read about fertilization, spraying, land,

wine-making, etc. Drive it, hike it and get to know it. Ask the (about his business plan. When you bring a buyer, you will know how to show it."

I asked Mimi if there were any properties she would *not sell.*

"I can't sell a property I don't like for some reason. This c; passed on to another realtor."

Then I asked Mimi to be specific. "Can you give me an examp a property you have refused to sell?"

Mimi replied, "I can't sell a cattle ranch that specializes in v(can't stand to think of those little babies in igloos that can neve outside. I can't eat veal and I can't sell that kind of property!"

I smiled. This was vintage Mimi. We have known Mimi fo years and have always regarded her as a friend with the highest etl standards. This kind of statement was typical of her. I think it sh(be a "mantra" for every salesperson. You should *sell only what believe in,* so you can sell with conviction and passion. Mimi is a cl; example of *getting high productivity without high pressure.*

To sum it all up, Mimi said,

- Take care of your people.
- You have a responsibility.
- Case out who your people are.
- Make sure they're not getting in over their heads.
- Your main job is to help and serve and make sure they don't get in trouble.
- Talk to them.
- Find out their interest.
- What is their objective?
- Then find the property that fits their need.

That is the essence of all successful selling, no matter what your field.

A bum steer—and a long wait

Not every real estate person is like Mimi. Let me tell you the kind of agent you should *NOT* use to sell your house. We had a beautiful 100-acre horse farm in New England. Mimi was in California so we could not use her. We had to look for a local real estate agent. We had restored the old New England farm home, built in 1791, and had added a gorgeous indoor equine facility with all the bells and whistles. We created new professionally landscaped gardens and riding trails. It was sensational. It was truly *unique*. (We learned later that "unique" is not a good thing in real estate!)

Our new real estate agent worked with a nationwide real estate agency that specialized in prestige properties. She was dazzled by all the wonderful things we had done to the property. It was the talk of the town. We had even been featured in *Town and Country* magazine. Our agent was sure she could get us a fabulous price, *more than any other property she had sold.*

Three years later, potential buyers continued to view and be dazzled by the splendor of the place, amazed at all we had done. We had lots of lookers and no contracts. The objections were typical. It was too far from the interstate (in Vermont)! It was too remote (small town, end of road location)! It did not have enough bedrooms, especially for a multi-million dollar property.

In reality, it was seriously overpriced and we did not have the experience to realize it. We wore rose-colored glasses when it came to our dream farm. Our real estate agent did not give us good advice. Finally, after three long and discouraging years, we sold it for half the original listing price. If our agent had given us good advice and priced it properly from the beginning, it would have sold in three or four months.

One thing we have learned on our own which our sales agent did not share with us is that the money invested in a property is not always returned to you when the property is sold. This is a basic fact in the real estate business. We were not in the real estate business and had no idea how true this principle is. Our agent was negligent in not giving

us the benefit of her knowledge. Her actions were self-serving (hoping for a huge commission). It would be generous to say that she also wore "rose-colored" glasses but I suspect the correct word for her was "incompetent". As for us, we were "gullible".

Years later my wife and I became real estate appraisers. As we studied our real estate appraisal courses, we shook our heads in dismay and disbelief at the mistakes we had made improving that property. It was "over improved", to say the least! It turned out to be by far the best property in the area, which is a huge "no-no" in real estate. Our original asking price was far higher than any other recent sale in the area. You've heard of "location, location, location," I'm sure. Our property was priced far outside the range of similar properties in the surrounding area. In fact, there were NO similar properties in the area. This should have sent us a warning flag but we were too inexperienced to see it. We can only guess at what our agent must have been thinking but not saying to us.

We had full confidence in our sales agent and her world-wide company. This confidence was completely misguided. She and her colleagues told us what we wanted to hear.

When you get ready to sell your own property, be as realistic as possible about its condition, age and especially about how it fits into the value of other properties in its neighborhood. This information and more is available to you as an individual seller through up-to-date online search engines and through your own town or county records. You do not have to rely on your sales agent to give you these basic facts, although it is always nice when you can!

A great real estate sales agent

A few years later, we were ready to move from New England to Georgia, where my wife and I had met 38 years earlier. First, though, we had to sell our beautiful, spacious condominium on the 16th hole of a first-class golf course. After the experience of selling our horse farm, we were now older and far wiser and wanted to price it to sell. We had a good idea of the price we could ask, comparing it with other condominiums recently sold in our community and throughout the entire city. We found a dynamic real estate sales team through word-of-mouth referrals. Jan and Fred knew the home sales market, our condominium complex with all its amenities and they knew what had to be done to sell an *expensive* property. (Notice that I said "*expensive*"—not "overpriced".)

They sold our condo within 24 hours after we signed their listing agreement! In fact, they sold it before the listing was even published in their own company directory!

Luck? Hardly. Jan and Fred were smart, organized and determined to put our condominium into the hands of a well-qualified buyer. They took their responsibilities under the listing contract as seriously as we did. To them, it wasn't just a tool to get our signatures on a commission agreement.

The importance of "staging" a home to sell was coming into its own at that time and Jan and Fred got it! They walked though our home with us, snapping digital photos, making notes, commenting on each room and what needed to be done to get our home ready to view.

"Steve, your eight grandchildren are just gorgeous but buyers don't want to see those photos. Pack them up and get them out of sight!"

"Your fireplace mantle looks so homey! Clear it off completely except for that antique Chinese vase".

"Keep fresh flowers in the living room at all times."

"Pack up three-quarters of your books. Leave only a few with beautiful bindings in view, interspersed with a few small decorative touches."

"Empty your kitchen cabinets of all but your most simple white dishes and best glassware."

"Put your thickest and most expensive towels in your master bath, add a green plant and a couple of fresh-smelling, pale-colored candles (unburned). Make it look like a spa. Freshen the upscale look every morning before your day begins and do the same with all the baths and half-baths."

"Empty those closets of most of the clothes. Leave only your basic wardrobe hanging. Pack up the pieces you intend to keep and put them in offsite storage. Give everything else away."

Was it successful? Do you call a two-day sale of a half-million dollar condo "successful?"

We had exactly two weeks to move out of our condominium and have it prepared for the new owners. We made it! After working with Jan and Fred, we felt that we could accomplish anything.

Savage Sales Secret #16

Sell with intelligence

I have bought dozens of cars over the years, but my most recent purchase highlights everything I have talked about in *Savage Sales Secrets*. I am going to tell you about two car dealers that completely blew a chance to sell me a luxury car—and another one who did it just right.

The first dealer blew his chance to sell us a car due to poor service over a two-year period. My wife likes to buy a car and keep it for several years. She had bought a fabulous Saab convertible from a great dealer who gave her great service. It was her favorite car of all time. She even liked it better than her Jaguar. In fact, the Jaguar sat in the garage so much that we finally sold it. She happily drove the Saab for 10 years and we moved away. We had to find another Saab dealer in the new city. It was no fun. Service was sloppy. Barrie would have driven the Saab for another ten years. But she did not like the Saab service department. It was time to trade.

We went to the Cadillac dealer. The salesperson took us straight out to the lot and stuck us in a lovely new Cadillac. We went for a ride while he talked the whole time. Yakkety yak. He never asked us what color we liked, what style we preferred or what we intended to use the car for. He was determined to sell that particular car. We asked him about financing. He said we would have to fill out an application before he could quote us on financing. We felt under a lot of pressure and got increasingly uncomfortable. Although the car was nice, it was not exactly what we wanted. The salesman annoyed us and we figured out a way to gracefully exit.

We had not thought about an Audi, but happened to drive by the Audi dealership. On impulse, we drove in. What a contrast to the Saab and Cadillac dealers! The showroom was large, clean, well-lighted and quiet. The salesman's name was Ralph. He asked us to sit down in two comfortable chairs across from his desk. He called us by name and asked us what type of car we were looking for. Size, color, use, business, pleasure. He covered everything quickly and efficiently. Then he said, "There are six cars here in the showroom. Why don't you go and sit in each one of them for a couple of minutes. Make sure you sit in both the front seat and the back seat. Then come back and tell me which one feels best."

What a great idea! We did precisely that. The Audi A8 was the roomiest car we had ever sat in since the good old days in the 50's and 60's when cars were *really* roomy. It was a truly full-size luxury executive car. We sat in the back seat and stretched our legs out—and pictured the comfort our families and friends would enjoy riding with us. I thought of my '57 Ford Fairlane back when I was in college! We were already half sold. We told Ralph we'd like to drive it.

When we drove it, he did not come with us. He simply handed us the keys and told us to have fun. We appreciated his low-keyed, easy-going, trusting manner. The big car hugged the road, felt wonderful on curves, purred along the interstate and blocked out almost all highway noise. It even had all-wheel drive. We were enchanted.

- Ralph was able to get *high productivity without high pressure.*
- He used a *soft* approach, a *soft* presentation and a *soft* close.
- He figured out what we needed and wanted, and got it for us.

Saab Story—"Sob" Story

My wife Barrie bought her first Saab convertible because the Saab mechanic sold her on it! It was the end of a day of car shopping and we were sick of car salespeople. Let me tell you what got us upset and then let me tell you about the Saab mechanic.

We wanted to buy a Dodge Viper. We had read all about it and were fascinated by its snarly good looks and its devilish presence. We lived in rural Vermont and the nearest Dodge dealer was an hour and a half away. We called and talked to a salesperson named Van. He was enthusiastic, of course, and told us he would love to give us a test drive in the Viper. We arranged and appointment and drove away.

When we got there, Van was not there. It was late in the day. No other salesperson was there. We called Van and tracked him down. He kept us waiting 30 minutes and finally showed up. No apology. Then, with great enthusiasm, he told us how much we were going to love the Viper and what a great trade-in we would get for our Chevrolet Suburban (which was a lot more practical in rural Vermont than a Viper)!

Van talked and talked. Yakkety yak. I finally interrupted and said I wanted to test drive the car. We finally got in and hit the road. The power was phenomenal. 0 to 60 in 4 seconds. I had never felt anything like it. 600 horsepower. I had never owned a sports car. I was giddy with excitement. I was ready to make a deal.

We got back and talked to Van. We said we were impressed and wanted to get a good trade-in on our Suburban which was only two years old. Well, Van could not give us a quote. Only the manager could do that. And the manager was not there! I was already irritated with Van for having kept us waiting. Now I was really annoyed. Van got in touch with the manager and arranged for us to come to the agency. In the meantime he kept talking about what a great deal the manager was going to give us.

The manager finally arrived and took our Suburban for a test drive. It was in perfect shape and had only 22,000 miles on it. Only two years old. We were about to buy a very expensive car. Then the bomb fell.

He quoted us about half what the Suburban was worth. We stormed out in disgust.

Van had wasted half a day of our time, driving to the agency, hanging around, talking nonsense and finally losing a sale. He had not prepared for the sale. He had not talked to his manager. He had a hot prospect. We were ready to buy. But through arrogance and stupidity, he lost the sale.

That's when we met the Saab mechanic.

It was getting dark. We were almost home. We had never considered a Saab. But as we passed the Saab dealership in Woodstock, Vermont, near our home, we decided to pull in. We had passed the place a thousand times. Only one person was there—Walt, the mechanic. We told him we just wanted to check and see what Saabs were like.

There was a convertible on the lot. Barrie had nursed a suppressed desire for a convertible ever since high school. In rural Vermont, a Saab convertible was just about as impractical as a Dodge Viper, but we had spent years driving 4-wheel drive vehicles. We were in an impractical mood.

Walt was your typical good old time Vermonter. He was the farthest thing from a flashy salesperson you can imagine. He just let us look at the car. He opened the hood. A sparkling clean engine. He opened the trunk. Perfection. Then he addressed the question that any Vermonter would have when considering a convertible. How does it stay warm in the winter when it is 40 below zero? We did not even have to ask the question. Walt answered it before we asked. He showed us how to put the top down. He said, "This convertible top is fully insulated and the seats are heated, so you'll be warm all winter long." *That was all we needed to hear.* Then he handed us the keys. We went for a test drive. It was fall in Vermont, and all the colors were ablaze: shrieking orange maple leaves, blazing red oaks, burning yellow willows. It was a magic evening. The convertible with the top down would not be practical much longer as the Vermont winter set in, but on this fall evening it was perfect. We were comforted to know it would be cozy even in the most brutal Vermont winter.

We returned and told Walt we wanted the car. He told us we'd have to come back in the morning to talk with the salesman, Jim. We did. When we met Jim, the only issue was the trade-in on the Suburban. Jim knew what it was worth. He did not have to consult with his manager. He offered us a fair price and in 15 minutes we had a deal.

Shortly after we arrived home, Van called from the Dodge dealership. He told us his manager had reconsidered and was willing to double the trade-in value on the Suburban. We laughed and told him we had just bought a Saab convertible. He was astonished.

The lessons here are obvious:

- You must be on time
- You must be prepared
- The salesperson must be able to make decisions
- You cannot waste the customer's time
- You must make it easy for the customer

The Saab dealer followed those five simple rules. The Dodge dealer did not.

But not all Saab dealers are created equal. Twelve years later, we were in a different city. We had moved away from our beloved Vermont. My wife does not trade cars often. She had kept her Saab convertible for 12 years. She would have kept it for another 12 years. But the Saab dealer in the new city had a terrible service department, unlike the meticulous service provided by Walt in Vermont. She decided it was time to trade.

Savage Sales Secret #17

Use names and even a bank can outsell the competition

We have done business with dozens of banks over the years. The friendliest and most customer-oriented is Wachovia. Every person, from the teller to the vice-president, calls you by name. At most banks, the drive-through is the most impersonal transaction of all. But not at Wachovia. When you drive in to make a deposit using the drive-through automated chutes, the teller receives your deposit and immediately calls you by name. "Good morning, Mr. Savage. Thank you for your deposit. Is there anything else you need today?"

"No, that's it for now."

"OK! Here's your deposit receipt. Have a wonderful day, Mr. Savage."

Whoosh! The cylinder rushes through the chute and I am off. She has used my name twice in 30 seconds and I feel good.

As I was writing this chapter I heard the news that Wachovia had been purchased by Wells Fargo. That was pretty good news, because Wells Fargo had been our bank when we had our business in California many years ago. Their service was good and we always liked Wells Fargo. However, Wachovia's customer service is the best I have ever seen and I hope their corporate culture sticks around!

Savage Sales Secret #18

Kill your competition with super service

My wife Barrie and I like to shop at Publix. They have about the same selection of food as other supermarkets. The layout is similar. The prices are about the same. But there is one big difference. *We rarely have to wait in line.*

Publix seems to have an uncanny ability to spot buildups of customers coming up to the cash registers. They quickly get extra cashiers in place. There is rarely more than one person ahead of you in line.

When you get to the cashier, you are always greeted with a smile. The cashier looks you in the eye, smiling, and asks, "Did you find everything you were looking for?" Then he or she quickly checks you out. There is almost always another person there to put your groceries in bags.

When the bagging is complete, the person always offers to take your cart out to the car. I always refuse the kind gesture, but am impressed with the offer.

From time to time I will go to another supermarket to buy groceries. I am spoiled. I am almost always annoyed when I have to wait in line because Publix has gotten me used to a fast checkout.

- Does your company make it easy and fast for your customers?
- Is it a pleasant experience to do business with you?
- If not, change your company culture immediately.
- Your sales and profits will soar.

Savage Sales Secret #19

Believe in yourself to become a champion

Champion belief sales secrets
Kyah Grady

When Kyah went to Western Washington University in Bellingham, she never dreamed she would spend the next nine summers selling books door-to-door! But when she heard about the incredible opportunity offered to college students, she jumped at the chance. Off she went, in June, 1997, along with other students from Western Washington, on a long drive east, across the Rocky Mountains and rolling prairies, to a five-day sales school run by the Southwestern Company in Nashville, Tennessee!

It was the Southwestern Company's genius to place students far away from home so they would have minimum distractions and maximum focus on sales. Kyah found herself that first summer assigned to Milford, Connecticut, 3,000 miles from home! She did not know a soul. There was nothing to do but work.

The company offered a "*Gold Award*" to any student who worked 80 hours a week, for 12 weeks, consistently, all summer long. Kyah was determined to win the award.

Each day she started work at 7:59 AM. That's right. Not 8:00 AM, but 7:59 AM. She focused herself on knocking on the first door at one minute before eight o'clock. And she did not quit until 9:30 PM, every day, six days a week, all summer long. She won the Gold Award but the real triumph was a personal one: she had proven to herself that she could enforce that kind of self-discipline and be completely relentless and tough-minded.

Her goal at the beginning of the summer was to sell 4,250 units. She beat that goal and sold 4,400 units for a personal profit of $17,500. She went back to Western Washington with enormous self confidence and optimism for her future.

Her second summer was a smashing success. She doubled her sales over her first summer, selling 9,800 units for a total profit of $49,000. Most people would have patted themselves on the back and been satisfied with those excellent results, but not Kyah. After her second successful summer, Kyah thought about the summer of '99. She thought about it every day. Way down deep, she made a personal commitment to herself: *to break the company record.*

The company record was 15,600 units. Kyah's goal was to beat it by 15 units. She spent the school year figuring out how she could sell 15,615 units.

> - She reflected, "I was dumb enough to believe I could do it. I felt that my best was like anyone else's best.
> - I kept thinking, 'You're as good as anyone else. Why not?'"

Kyah wrote her thoughts and goals on paper. She reflected on speeches she had heard and books she had read. Her notes to herself included pithy philosophies that spoke to her heart:

- If it can be done on paper, it can be done.
- Most people work on minimums, not on maximums. I'm going to work on maximums.
- I'm at least as good as everyone else out there and maybe even better, so why hold myself back?

Kyah told me, "The job is so mental. There are tons of people who are smarter and more intuitive than I, but they never allow themselves to break out. Most people compete with the averages. Why not compete with the best?"

I kept probing, asking Kyah about her sales techniques, thinking I would discover a magic phrase or a secret close, but her replies were quite basic. "I just memorized the sales talks and believed they would work. A lot of other student dealers did not believe those closes would work and invented their own. I just kept repeating the lines that other successful people had used. I listened, asked questions and let the customers talk and vent. I think that's why people liked to do business with me."

The third summer she put all her positive mental energy in place and focused on breaking the company record. She determined to make each hour her very best hour. She was relentless in making each minute count. By the end of the summer, she had sold 17,200 units and earned $86,000. She was a hero at Southwestern and an unbelievable success story back home and at school.

The average person would be content to break a record and rest on her laurels. But Kyah is not your average person. She spent the next nine months thinking about the summer of 2000. She thought she could break her own record.

It was her senior year. She focused on three things: studies, recruiting and her own personal sales. Every day she thought about ways that she could beat her own personal record. She considered minutes that she had rested in the middle of the day and decided not to take any more breaks. She wrote down her goals and made her plans.

The summer of 2000 arrived. Kyah graduated from Western Washington and took a team of students across the country to Nashville, Tennessee. She got them trained and worked with them every Sunday. But from Monday through Saturday she was relentlessly, totally absorbed with her own personal sales, from 7:59 AM to 9:30 PM. By the end of the summer, she had indeed broken her own record: 18,600 units for a personal profit of $93,000!

After Kyah finished college, she kept selling every summer for five more summers! She became a sales manager with Southwestern and was responsible for recruiting, training and leading a group of 60 to 100 students each summer. She moved to Southern California and recruited students at UCLA and Point Loma Nazarene College in San

Diego. During the summers, she led by example, continuing to sell and setting the example for her trainees. Usually someone was with her, running and gasping, trying to keep up with her.

During the summer of 2001, she was able to sell for only 8 weeks instead of her normal 12 weeks. The other weeks, she was busy training her student dealers. Thus, she did not break her total record for an entire summer. But she did break two new company records: most sales for one day (615 units, $3,075 profit) and most sales in one week (2,750 units, $13,750 profit). She sold 15,600 units in 8 weeks for a total personal profit of $78,000. Even though she was unable to work a full 12-weeek summer, this was her most productive summer in terms of earnings per week.

I asked her how she had done so much in only 8 weeks. She replied that during previous summers she would get a cup of coffee in the middle of the afternoon to rejuvenate herself. Sometimes she would call her sales manager in Nashville. But in the summer of 2001, she decided, "I'm not going to talk to anyone except Mrs. Jones. I didn't touch the phone. I didn't touch a cup of coffee. I wanted to see what I could do. I didn't have a single second to spare."

Kyah said it was hard to imagine going into the corporate world after nine summers in the "book field." She was a genuine "guerrilla." She saw many of her friends go into the corporate world after college, but she never envied them a bit. She had wings and was flying.

I said to Kyah, "I know you worked hard. But a lot of other people also worked hard. What did you do differently to make you number one?"

Kyah replied, "It was a combination of things. One of the things that spurred me on was one of the other student managers who told me I couldn't do it. That really got under my skin! His words ate at me as I got mentally ready for the summer.

"Then I broke it down into numbers. If I do 18 sit-downs a day instead of 17 and if I have this closing percentage and if I have this average package size, then I'll do this amount of dollars. It came out to 18,200 units. It's easy on paper to see how it can be done. I know I'm good at establishing rapport. I know I'm good at reading people in an interview situation.

"I went to every single motivational class and absorbed the words like 'successful people do the things that failures don't like to do.' Whenever I was on a treadmill, I was pushing myself harder on the last few laps than I had the day before. So I knew I was prepared.

"A lot of people don't allow themselves to be successful. Many folks think, 'I'll at least get by.' I never thought that way. I always wanted to do *this much*, so I could never get complacent out there. My goal was so high that I couldn't just say, 'Oh, well, I only sold two today.' I have been on both sides of that emotional coin, so I understand people who feel that 'I'll just get by' but now I was determined to keep my mind focused so I would never think that way.

I kept wondering when Kyah would start talking about her sales techniques, but the conversation kept moving along on her mind set. Finally I asked, "Do you think it's a mental thing and not a technique thing?"

Kyah responded, "People tell me I'm so good, and honestly, I don't even think that way. Some people are very technical and they also get great results by describing their sales techniques. I can tell you how I do it, but I don't like to break it down like that. I just do it and don't like to think about why I do it. I've had people follow me around and tell me my technique is just like theirs. I just follow the sales talk we learned in Nashville.

"I have an outline in my head. I ask them questions. Then I steer them down this funnel. Then we come to the decision and I've hardly said anything.

> • "They answer a few questions. I let them talk and talk and talk. Then I say, 'Well, that's why people have been getting this.' It doesn't matter what they say. They feel like you've listened.
> • "I always think I can. I think I can close the deal. I just know it will happen.

"There are people who compete on an A level. Others compete on a B level and others on a C level. If a person thinks as a 'B' then they look at other 'B' level people and compete with them. Anybody can compete at an A level. But most people won't allow themselves to think that way.

"After I finished my career as a sales manager, I sold insurance for Southwestern's insurance company, Family Heritage Life Insurance Company. I was in Texas. I had never sold insurance before. I used the same technique. By Tuesday night I had sold 600 units. No one had ever done that before. My feeling was, 'I'm not messing around. I've got work to do.' On Wednesday they had someone else follow me around. She had never sold more than 200 units a week. Now she is selling 1200 to 1500 units per week. She realized, 'You know, I can do this!' It's all mentality.

I repeated, "Kyah, you haven't told me about your pre-approach, your approach, your presentation or your close. Is it all mental?"

"Yeah, I guess it is. I don't know how you teach that to somebody. People have to grasp the concept and run with it. Obviously, I had soaked up everything I could possibly learn. It wasn't as though I was out there saying anything that came into my mind. Some people get good at the approach. Others get good at the close. I decided to get good at everything. I wanted it all.

"When I knocked on a door, I had the feeling, 'I am supposed to be here. I was sent here to help you and to help your kids.' That gave me enormous self-confidence."

"Was there anything you did that was different from the others in your pre-approach, your approach, your presentation or your close?"

"One day one of the experienced salespeople followed me around for the whole day. About half way through the day, he commented, 'Wow! You really use the close—to close!' That amazed me! I did not know there was any other way to do it. It was so simple. Our sales talk was so straight forward: 'Mrs. Jones, that's what everyone likes about the way I do business. I'm just here taking orders today. I'll deliver the books at the end of the summer. That way, if you were to get a set, you wouldn't have to pay for it all at one time. That would be pretty cool, huh?'"

Kyah kept selling and managing until 2005. Then Dustin Hillis came along. Let's talk about him next.

No mental barriers sales secrets

Dustin Hillis

Imagine earning $100,000 in one summer as a college student! Dustin Hillis holds the all-time record of the 150-year-old Southwestern Company of Nashville, Tennessee. I told you in the first chapter of this book that I worked my way through college selling books back in the early 60's. Dustin broke into the 21st century and broke barriers that we never dreamed of back in the 60's.

One person that motivated Dustin was Kyah, who had shattered all company records the previous summer. Dustin began to talk with Kyah on the phone to find out her secrets. She was generous with her information, not quite realizing that Dustin's dream was to break her record. When he blasted through the hurdle she had raised, she accepted it graciously but competitively. They remained friendly competitors, and got better acquainted. Their friendship blossomed into romance and now they are married, building and growing together.

After talking with Kyah, with her unbelievable positive attitude, I asked Dustin how he had ever beaten her record. She had made $93,000 in one summer. It seemed like an almost unbeatable record. But not for Dustin.

First, he talked to Kyah on the phone. He picked her brain and tried to figure out all the things she had done to break through previous barriers. He knew he had a great closing ratio, but was not getting in as many doors as Kyah. So, as a first step, he decided he had to get in at least 90% of the doors. This meant he could not simply make a demonstration at the door. He had to get in, sit down and get the customer relaxed. When they were relaxed, he was confident he could sell most of them. He knew he had a product they needed. If they had kids in school, his books would help them get better grades. Armed with that confidence, he spent nine months thinking about his next summer, just like Kyah had done two years earlier.

Dustin reflected, "I was working 85 hours a week, making 30 to 40 demonstrations a day. I could not work any harder. But I needed to get better results. I needed to become a professional and do something dramatically different.

"My first summer was 2002. I was #1 with 7,000 units. My second summer I had 9,000 units.

"My third summer I decided to break the record. One of my guiding philosophies was that I was going to get into 90% of the doors I knocked on. I had a great closing ratio, but I wasn't getting enough *sit-downs*. I was closing one out of two—a 50% closing ratio. That came from knowing when they crossed the "buying line" rather than closing too soon or talking too much."

"My first two summers, I didn't know my sales talk very well. I had very little product knowledge. I remembered Dan Moore saying in sales school, "When they go above the buying line, close right then." So, if I saw a person raise his eyebrows, look at the book and make a positive comment, I knew it was time to close."

"That was enough to do pretty well my first two summers. That got me by, but it wasn't enough to break the record. For my third summer, I decided I wanted to break the record which Kyah had set in 2000. 18,600 units. No one had broken it in three summers. The summer of 2004 was coming up.

"I decided to do two things:

1. I was going to get in 90% of the doors.
2. I was going to be a student of the game.

"The first two summers, I was winging it. I knew the close. I had it memorized. As far as the product, I didn't know it as well as I should. But now it was time to get intimately acquainted with the product."

"My student manager, who had sold books for 7 years, followed me around for a day at the end of my second summer. I sold 290 units that day. He said to me, 'It's astonishing. You have no idea what you're doing, but you sold more books today than I have ever sold in one day in 7 summers! If you ever figure out what you're doing and take this seriously, you're going to blow away the record.'

"That was the first time the seed was planted in my mind that it was even possible and I had even thought about it. So, as I was driving home that summer from the book field, I was consumed by that thought. I could break the record set by Kyah in 2000. She had sold 18,600 units and I had sold only 9,000 units. I had to more than double my sales to beat her.

"Now, 9,000 units is not a shabby summer, but it wasn't my best. That's when I made a decision, and it was a clear, defining moment in my life. I said, 'I need to take this seriously.' I thought that if I broke the record, it would open up all kinds of doors for me in the future. That motivated me.

"My second summer I was in Canton, Texas, southeast of Dallas. At the end of the summer, as I drove 14 hours back to Nashville, I was figuring out how I could break the record my third summer. It was the beginning of my junior year. I kept thinking about it and thought that there was no logical reason why I could not do it."

"My first summer I was #1 among the first-year dealers. My second summer I was #3 in the whole company, but I was the #1 second-year dealer."

"After my second summer, as part of my strategy to become a student of the game of selling, while attending University of Tennessee in Knoxville, I switched my major from Business to Psychology. It was my junior year in college. I became a serious student. The results from that affected me more than just me being able to sell more effectively. Also, my GPA went up. I decided to become a professional in everything I did."

"I hand wrote my sales talk, every single word. I actually enjoyed breaking down a 150-year-old sales talk. As I was writing it out I was thinking, "Why am I saying what I am saying?" "What are they thinking when I say every single word in my whole entire sales talk?"

"I read books, listened to CD's and attended sales courses throughout the school year. I took copious notes. When I got back to my room I would take my notes and condense them to one page. Then I organized my notes in terms of the cycle of the sale: Pre-approach, approach, introduction, presentation, answering objections, closing and referrals. I had every CD Southwestern had ever made...about 30 CD's in all. Kyah had recorded three CD's. All the record holders before her had CD's."

"Then as I went through my notes, I plugged in all these advanced ideas specifically into the areas where they applied. One idea I got was the "Dad Approach." Whenever a Dad came to the door, I would say, "I don't want to waste your time." That got the Dads relaxed so I could talk with them. I scripted an entire "Dad Approach" and built that into the sales talk.

"Our sales talks did not go into the topic of 'what to say to kids.' But on all these advanced sales CD's, there were lots of ideas. I developed three questions that I put to kids. They were sitting there with their Mom, looking at my books. I then said, "OK, I want you to look at these books and then I'm going to ask you three questions when we're done. And I want you to tell your parents the answers to these questions, too, because it's important."

The kids would say "OK."

"First of all I want you to tell me whether you think this is something that will help you save time on your homework. Second, I want to make sure you feel it is something that will help you whenever you get stuck. And, third, I want to be sure you feel it's something you will use. Because if you don't use it, then it's not worth your parents' time or money to invest in this. But if you will use it, then it's worth your parents investing in it, because there is nothing more important than your kids' education.

"That is such a great series of questions! The kids would say 'OK' and the parents would say 'OK.' But that had never been scripted anywhere. So I took all the verbiage I had heard from other successful salespeople and all the things I had said as I was winging it out there and literally scripted all of that. I made it into an advanced sales talk."

"These are the same concepts I still teach today when coaching people. Most people know what to do or say. They have read it in a book, heard it on a CD, or listened to their manager or a speaker at a conference talk about working referrals, answering objections, staying motivated, and staying focused while working consistently on a good schedule. What I find is that *most people just do not do what they know they should do*! Doing what was on the advanced sales CD's was the paradigm shift for me. This I find is what separates top producers from average producers. Accountability and application are what I coach and train people on today."

"One of the Critical Success Factors for me to break the company record was to apply the advanced techniques into the "Sales Cycle". I broke down the entire cycle of the sale and analyzed each step:

- **Pre-approach:** Get people's names from the neighbors and find out what time they were home and what grade their kids were in.

- **Approach:** Know what to say at the door so they will be relaxed and invite you in.

- **Introduction:** Get seated and relaxed. Finding their need and creating a "buying atmosphere".

- **Presentation:** Talk about their "hot buttons" by asking engaging questions and showing them how the books will help their kids in school.

- **Answering objections:** Don't argue. Agree with the objection so the customer is relaxed. Mention someone else who felt the same way. Then tell them how that person resolved the question to their satisfaction.

- **Close:** Make it easy for them to buy by giving them a choice between "yes" and "yes" and close on minor points.

- **Referrals:** Ask based on "who you know." Who would be a good person for me to go talk to about helping their kids out with educational needs? Just like we finished doing with you here today.

"Working referrals was another Critical Success Factor for me on my record breaking summer. My goal was to know the first name, what time they were home, and the grade of their kids for at least 80% of the doors I knocked on. This was a huge step in getting in 90% of the doors I knocked on!"

"I kept thinking, 'What are the people thinking as I say something?' For example, I would say, 'Most people think these are really expensive like a set of encyclopedias or a set of college textbooks.' So I'm thinking that they are thinking, 'Yeah, these are gonna be expensive, too.' So I put myself in their shoes throughout the whole sales talk. That way, by the time I got to sales school at the beginning of the summer, I not only knew my sales talk but I knew what was going on in the customers' minds, and I knew how to answer the objections they might have before they ever had a chance to get them out of their mouth."

"When we got to sales school, I played a game where instead of doing 30 demos, which is what most people in sales school are thinking and talking about, I told the other student dealer to whom I was making the demo to *not* buy. 'Act like a real parent that I am going to run into this summer who is really close minded and negative and I want you to give me every objection that's in the book.' I did 30 during sales school. By the time I had done 15 or 20 I was killing it. Even the student dealers, my friends, who knew all the objections, couldn't say no.

At this point, Kyah chimed in. One thing that is important to me to clarify is that I knew Dustin was going for my record and I believed he could do it. Another sales manager had told me, "I don't think Dustin can do it, it's only his 3rd summer." And I told him, "Why not? I broke the record my 3rd summer. There's a good chance he can do it if he thinks he can."

Dustin smiled and continued, "My first week I sold 1,300 units. Before that, my best week had been 1,100 units. I knew the foundation had been laid and I was on track to break the record."

Then Dustin got serious again.

> • "One of the common denominators of success is that you do things that other people don't enjoy doing.
> • Successful people form the habit of doing daily the things that unsuccessful people do not like to do."

"This was the famous quote by **Albert Gray** that has always inspired me."

"That was a huge revelation for me. I used to say, 'I don't like this' or 'I don't like that.' Then I discovered that you don't necessarily have to like something in order to do it."

"You hear people say this all the time: 'I don't feel like doing it because I don't like it.' Or they will say 'I don't want to commit to setting my goals too high because I don't think it's realistic'. My favorite, though, is, 'I could have done it if I really wanted to!' If I gave into the mind set of being average and having average thoughts like those I would have stopped after having my best week ever my first week on the field; and if I didn't break the record I could have said "I did my best. I still sold more than I did the previous year." But when it comes down to it I truly believe that the people who make it in life actually do what they say they are going to do."

I asked Dustin, "Where were you the summer you broke the record?"

"West Texas, in the Amarillo area. I sold in 13 small towns in the panhandle of Texas. God Bless Texas!"

Then Dustin got extra serious. He confided, "Steve, if you want to know how I do what I do, let me put it to you as clearly as I can. The credit for my success goes to God and to other people in my life. My Dad said I could do anything if I put my mind to it. He was right. That phrase is one of my earliest memories. My mentors were God, my Dad (Steve Hillis), and my Grandfather (Gene Caughron). I felt closest to God when I was selling books. It was important for me to be balanced spiritually."

"When I was selling books was always when I was closest to God. It's just you out there making a difference. I was out in the desert of West Texas. I felt like I was balanced spiritually."

"It was also the healthiest time for me. I wasn't drinking. I was doing pushups and sit-ups every day. I think that had a big part to play. I was thinking clearly. By the end of the summer I was doing 120 pushups a day. My goal was to do one more every day and always be competing with myself. Often I was running so far ahead of the pack that I had to create these self-competitions. I always wanted to beat myself by a little bit. So I'd start my morning by doing one more push up or one more sit-up every day. That really helped me keep that mental edge on myself. Competing with myself is the toughest competition I have found."

"I ate healthy food. I didn't take many breaks. One thing about Kyah: she could work a lot more efficiently than I. She could do it in less time. I had to put in the numbers to make my system work."

"How many hours did you work each day?"

"14 to 14 ½."

"When did you start and when did you finish each day?"

"I started at 7:30 AM and worked until 10:00 or 10:30 PM. My average was 85 hours per week."

"How many demonstrations did you make each day?"

"This was another shift from my second summer to my third. My third summer I focused only on '*sit-downs.*' I stopped recording useless activity. I said to myself, 'Why the heck am I doing 40 demonstrations a day?' I can tell the customer, 'Look at the book!' And nothing happens. So I made sure I got in the door and sat down with the customer. I set my goal to do 20 'sit-downs' every day."

"So the ones you did standing outside the door were not that productive?"

"No. I *did* have a door demo. If I did a door demo, it was to sell them the books. So many people do a door demo just so they can say they did X number of demos that day, to make themselves feel good. That's the dumbest thing I've ever heard of. So I actually scripted a door demo as part of my strategy I was telling you about. My goal was to have the world's best door demo. If I could not get a sit-down, I was going to sell them the books. Every day or every other day I would sell at least one door demo. I'd still sell 35 or 36 units, even in my door demo.

"Sometimes I'd use my door demo to get a sit-down. I'd start the demo and then say, 'You know, this only takes about 5 minutes. Do you have a place we could sit down so you can see it more easily?' Often that converted a door demo to a sit-down.

"By the end of the summer, I was getting an average of 23 calls and 21 sit-downs per day. Before I got to the door, I knew their name and their kids' names. I knew how to navigate through the approach. So I stopped doing 30 demos. I wasn't even knocking on 30 doors."

"So 20 sit-downs was your goal?"

"Yes."

"And 20 sit-downs would take 14 hours?"

"Yes. When I teach the experienced sales dealers in the Top Producer Club, I just flat out tell them that demos don't count. Only sit-downs count. This is what a lot of my book "Navigate: Selling the Way People Like to Buy" is about; how to emotionally connect with someone at the door or on the phone and have them like you and trust you quickly. I found that by understanding how to identify peoples' buying behavior styles and adapt my selling style to match their buying style. It gave me a huge advantage on getting in the door.

- Dustin's book *Navigate* can be found at http://secure.ssnseminars.com/store/Development-Resources-C10.aspx

I asked Dustin, "You've talked a lot about techniques. You've also talked a lot about belief. Which is more important?"

Dustin replied, "Probably belief. There was nothing that could stop me. You could have cut my leg off and I would have cut down a tree, whittled it down into a peg leg, and kept selling. I just convinced myself that I could break the record and nothing was going to stop me."

As I interviewed Dustin, I found an interesting parallel with my talk with Kyah. Even though each of them spoke about sales techniques, they both talked more about mental attitude.

Dustin talked about the *"belief barrier."*

- *You don't understand 'no' or 'don't'*
- *You don't understand how something can't be done. You see no walls.*
- *You do things that other people don't do."*

"Henry Bedford (Southwestern's CEO) has told me that what inspires him about hanging out with me is that I don't have a belief barrier. He told me, 'You don't understand *no*. You don't understand how to not figure something out. You don't understand when somebody tells you something can't be done. You have no barriers. You see no walls. Everything is an answer for you.'

"Henry always encourages me to keep doing that, because I can be frustrating to people from time to time. If someone wants me to see the 'reality of a situation' or 'the reason something cannot be done' I often will give them a blank stare and reply with "why not?""

I laughed and said to Dustin, "You have no barriers. Kyah has no barriers. You see no walls. Kyah sees no walls. Here you guys are in your beautiful condo on the top floor of this building overlooking Nashville. What keeps you two from flying through the roof?

We all laughed.

Neither Dustin nor Kyah needed to use high pressure.

- They got high productivity without high pressure because they believed in themselves and in their product,
- They were focused yet relaxed
- They allowed the customer to talk.

Dustin put it all into practice in the summer of 2004. Kyah's record of 18,600 units had stood like Mount Everest since 2000. She had earned $93,000 in one summer, an unbelievable amount for a college kid. But Dustin was ready to conquer that mountain. His goal was to sell more than 20,000 units and earn over $100,000.

His first week he sold 1,300 units. That was good, but not nearly enough to sell 20,000 units in 14 weeks. He ramped it up, making each minute of each 14 ½ hour day count, with focused intensity, sheer belief in himself and no doubts.

His best days were rainy days. Those were days that got most salespeople off track. They motivated Dustin to run from his car to the door and get inside the house! He had one week where he sold over 2,500 units. Kyah had sold 2,750 units in one week back in 2001. She had sold 615 units in one day. Those were still company records and Dustin was never able beat her on those two records. But overall, as the summer marched on, he advanced on her summer-long record. By the end of 14 weeks, he had sold 20,200 units and earned over $100,000!

Dustin and Kyah, the fierce competitors, were both extraordinary winners. They had immense respect and admiration for each other. As they shared each other's victories and the euphoria of triumph, those feelings blossomed into romantic passion. It was better than a fairy tale. The two champions were married in 2005!

I jokingly asked Kyah how the fierce rivalry could have evolved into a happy marriage. She laughed and said, "No problem. If you can't beat 'em, join 'em!"

Seminar sales secrets

Success Starts Now!

After Dustin graduated from the University of Tennessee with a B.A. in Psychology, he got together with two other top Southwestern Company graduates: Gary Michels and Rory Vaden. They saw a very special opportunity to build a company that combined sales training seminars with sales consulting. They did not want to waste time and become successful in several years. They wanted success—*now*! So, quite aptly, they named their company *Success Starts Now*! www.ssnseminars.com

Success Starts Now! was formed as a new business under the Southwestern Company family of companies. Their goal was "to help salespeople become top producing sales professionals and break through the personal belief barriers and achieve the goals of their dreams."

Ticket sales secrets

I observed their team in action a month before a seminar in Chicago. It was fascinating to see the way they sold tickets. I have been in the seminar business for many years, but have never seen such a powerful effort at selling tickets.

The team had a database of companies with sales forces. In many cases, they had the name of the sales manager or vice president of sales. They had phone numbers. The key was to get in touch with the person who could make a decision to let them come and conduct a free workshop for all the salespeople.

Telephone sales secrets

The critical first phone call has one objective: get in front of all the salespeople so you can sell them tickets to the seminar.

Who will give you permission to talk to the salespeople? In a large company, it could be the VP of sales. In a small company, it would most likely be the owner.

Your offer is tantalizing: a *free workshop for the salespeople* with no obligation and no strings attached. Naturally, you want to sell tickets, but there is no commitment to buy any minimum. It is totally voluntary.

You get in touch with the VP of sales and you tell him or her that you will be having a fantastic seminar in a few weeks. "In order to give your sales team an idea of what the seminar is all about, we are offering a *free 45-minute workshop* which will give them guaranteed techniques on the approach, the presentation and the close. What time would be most convenient for you to have the workshop?"

Most sales managers like the idea of a free workshop. They want their salespeople to get more training. So, they often agree to do the workshop.

Workshop Sales Secrets

The workshop is an honest-to-goodness teaching seminar. It is not merely a sales pitch for the seminar. The sales manager and the sales people feel enriched with solid, down-to-earth selling principles that will help every person in the room improve his or her sales performance.

At the end, of course, there is a description of the seminar coming up. The salespeople are asked, "How many of you have learned something this morning that will help you in your sales this week?" They usually raise their hands. "Well, this is merely a taste of what you will get at the seminar." Then the workshop leader goes on to describe in detail the topics that will be covered in the seminar including:

- What Separates Top Producers from Average Producers
- Selling to Different Behavioral Types
- The Secrets of Self-Motivation
- Industrial Strength Sales Strategies
- 12 Different Types of Closes
- How To Be Funny to Make More Money
- Selling to the Sexes
- Handling Objections and Excuses
- Cracking the Code of Cold Calling

Using these techniques, the Workshop Leaders are able to sell 500 to 1,000 tickets per seminar.

During and after the seminar, many of the participants sign up for continuing sales coaching and consulting programs, expertly led by the team of professionals, most of whom have come through the Southwestern summer book selling program.

Dustin says there are four top reasons salespeople choose the Success Starts Now! programs.

"First, it's different. It's new and fresh. We use experts from a variety of sales disciplines.

"Second, we rely on technique as well as motivation. When techniques are used successfully, they instill confidence in a salesperson. Motivation comes as a natural bi-product.

"Third, salespeople can relate to our staff. We are not personality driven, but rather principle driven. Our team is trained on the best practices of over 250,000 "sales guerillas" who came before us, and that is what we teach. We are young enough to connect to the new generation of salespeople, but experienced enough to shed new light on issues that most experienced sales professionals grapple with.

"Fourth, we take into account different personality types when offering our techniques. We provide a variety of ways to approach a single issue: soft handed, mild, assertive and industrial strength. The program is not about one system or philosophy. It's all about what really works and what doesn't work in today's marketplace."

For more details about Success Starts Now! and personal sales coaching and sales training events go to www.ssnseminars.com.

Follow your passion sales secrets
Kyah becomes a fashion stylist

Kyah Hillis has pursued her lifelong dream of becoming a fashion consultant and stylist. She knew she could take all the techniques she had learned in selling books and apply them to the field she had dreamed about all her life: fashion. Her story will inspire you, because when *Savage Sales Secrets* become a part of your life, you also will be able to follow your dreams and do whatever you have always longed to do.

Dustin Hillis followed his passion and formed the seminar company Success Starts Now! with his two partners. Meanwhile Kyah tried a couple of sales jobs, with great success, but all along, she was haunted by the sense that she was missing out on her own passion: style and design. She had always dressed fashionably, even as a college student dashing from house-to-house selling books. Now, Dustin and Kyah were living in Nashville, Tennessee, the home of country music. Kyah thought to herself, "Here are all these country music singers, needing someone who understands fashion, to get them prepped for photo shoots and make sure they look great when they get on stage. All I have to do is combine my love for fashion with my good old-fashioned sales skills, and I'm in business!"

She gathered together all her knowledge of sales that she had learned in the book business: pre-approach, approach, presentation and close. Most of all, she gathered up her emotional strength that had made her believe in herself and catapulted her into record-holder for top sales in one summer. As she had told me earlier, it was all mental. She believed she could be the best at selling books. Now, she believed she could be a terrific fashion consultant. Not an ordinary fashion consultant, but an outstanding one.

As you read Kyah's story, and other stories in this book, think about your own passion. What do you want more than anything else? Are you stuck in a rut? Do you long to get out of what you're doing so you can pursue your dreams? Just do it! Follow Kyah and Dustin and all these proven *Savage Sales Secrets* and you can do it too!

So now, picture Kyah leaving behind the safe world she knows so well and where she has been so successful. She knows a lot about fashion and she knows how to dress and look fabulously stylish. But she has never approached anyone about styling. She developed a marketing plan even before she started making phone calls. She felt there were *three areas where she could fill a need and help people.* (And that is the secret to success in any sales business!)

1. Help individuals who need professional assistance in designing their wardrobe.
2. Help coordinate and produce fashion shoots for magazines and advertising agencies.
3. Help artists, especially musicians, put together a fabulous wardrobe.

Boldly, she set forth on *Step #1* and contacted a few people she knew personally who had excellent clothes, but lacked the magic touch to put them all together in a fashionable way. This took tact, courage and finesse. After chatting with various folks, she realized there were two types of prospects within this category:

1. Those who needed help building an entire wardrobe.
2. Those who needed monthly assistance in choosing two or three outfits each month.

Kyah quickly got her first customer reorganized. She had lots of clothes that did not tie together. Kyah picked out the belts, jewelry, shoes and accessories that made everything click. Her customer immediately looked stunning, was thrilled and began to refer her friends to Kyah.

Kyah knew that she needed to develop a website in order to tangle with the well-established high fashion stylists, so she picked a great name and immediately got a professional look that was "feminine but edgy."

http://www.panachestylists.com/

She also began a blog that was linked to her website and signed it, *Kyah, your Fashion Stylist*. This gave her a *brand and an identity*.

www.theivoryfeather.blogspot.com

The blog is upscale, sophisticated and cool. Now, she had a website, a blog, some experience, a few referrals and was ready to tangle with the "big boys." She was ready for *Step #2 in her marketing plan: fashion photo shots*. She went straight to the premier magazine in Nashville, the only glossy magazine in the area. **Nashville Life Styles** covers restaurants, fashions and life styles. She offered her services as a stylist for fashion photo shots. They liked her self-confidence, her *"feminine but edgy"* look, her blog and her referrals. They said, "OK, we'll give you a try."

She found a great photographer, a terrific make-up artist, an ideal location, and organized the whole event. In essence, she became the producer and the director. She did not limit herself to the notion that she was a "fashion consultant." She did whatever it took to get the job done. In the end, the photo shoot was a dramatic success.

Since then, she has gotten numerous jobs with **Nashville Life Styles** and has worked with several photographers and make-up artists. As she has gotten to know these folks, she has teamed up with the two or three best in each profession. She can call on them whenever she gets a job, assemble a first-class team and jump into action. She was recently featured on the cover of **W25**, a national online fashion magazine.

Think about what Kyah has done. *She has followed her passion.* She has been bold enough to jump into a new arena and assert herself. She has refused to accept any mental barriers. The principles that made her successful as a college student selling books door-to-door are now making her successful as a fashion stylist.

Kyah was now ready to move on to Step #3 in her marketing plan: *working with artists.* She lived just a few blocks from the Grand Old Opry, so this was a perfect opportunity. She knew she had to get herself face-to-face with music label producers, managers and the singers themselves. Does this sound scary to you? Well, Kyah is tough mentally, but like all of us, she gets scared.

- *No one likes to make cold calls.*
- *No one likes rejection.*
- But to become a great salesperson, you need to understand one of the fundamental *Sales Secrets* of all time:
- *You don't take rejection personally.*
- *And you just go out and do it.*

Armed with her portfolio of previous photo shoots she had done, she went directly to the manager of a record label and said, "I want to organize your next photo shoot. Here is what I have done for **Nashville Life Styles.** I style the shoot. If needed, I can compile a whole team and scout locations. I organize the photographer, the make-up artist, the location, everything. Just leave it up to me and we will make your artist look like a star." In essence, she can provide a package deal for the creative director of a label. She can simply do her job as fashion stylist, or provide a whole team. It is her flexibility and creativity that give her added value and a special edge.

Kyah then developed relationships with the high-style fashion stores in Nashville. They would give her up to several thousand dollars worth of clothes on consignment, based on the relationship and trust she had established. She would take them to the photo shoot, try different outfits on the artist and take awesome pictures. Often, the label manager would wind up buying clothes for the artists, so the local store was happy and Kyah developed a network of contacts throughout the city.

Kyah has developed a relaxed attitude about her job. She says, "I don't have to get every job. I need to get the jobs that are right for me. I define the esthetic and people come to me." Earlier, Kyah had told me that her name meant "life" in Hebrew and "peace" in Hawaiian. I told her, "Kyah, you are getting the most out of *life* by fulfilling your dream and you are at *peace* with yourself." She agreed.

I asked her how she made her first contact with a Creative Director at a record label. First, she used a mailing in which she sent samples of her work. Then she followed up with a phone call, designed to get her face-to-face with her customer. Her typical phone call goes something like this: "Hi, this is Kyah, the fashion stylist. Did you get the package I sent you? Great! I'm going to be in your area tomorrow. I was wondering if I could drop by for a few minutes around 11 am or if tomorrow afternoon around 2 PM would be more convenient for you?"

- This is the classic choice of "yes" or "yes."
- It is the best way to get *high productivity without high pressure.*
- It works for Kyah.
- It will work for you.

Savage Sales Secret #20

Be grateful for your profession as a salesperson

The Southwestern Company today

When I was one of eighteen sales managers back in 1966-1960, each of us lived in Nashville. We each had an office in the Southwestern Company headquarters but we spent nine months of the year traveling to college campuses across the country. During the summer, we were in the office every day, dictating letters and talking to salespeople on the phone. On Sunday afternoons, we traveled out to have sales meetings wherever we had our people selling. Each of us managed between 150—400 students.

My territory was vast—the Midwest and the West Coast. I loved it, because I got to open up new schools. The Southwestern Company had been concentrated in the South and Southwest for most of its history. I was on the cutting edge of new frontiers.

How things have changed! Nate Vogel is a great example. He has been with Southwestern for 22 years. He attended Western Washington in Bellingham and now lives near Seattle, Washington. He spends most of his year on the West Coast, recruiting, just like I did, but he is close to home. My home was in Nashville, but when traveling throughout the West Coast for recruiting, my home was in hotels! I envied Nate's model.

Nate had the privilege of managing Kyah, whom I talked about in the last chapter, watching her become the #1 student dealer in the company. He was her leader for eight summers, watching her develop until she broke the company record.

Our old model was simply Division Vice President, Sales Manager and Student Manager. A Student Manager could develop an organization with several layers, but essentially his or her job was over once they graduated from college.

Now there is a different structure. Nate has 250 students in his organization, just like I did 40 years ago. But the number of units they sell is exponentially higher. Back in the 60's and 70's, a student who made $1,500 in their first summer was considered awesome. Today a student can earn more than that at McDonald's! It's a different world. Thus, an average student will now make $6,000 in the first summer. The top first year student last year was Ilene Reid of the University of Washington. She earned $23,724!

Nate also managed the #2 overall student dealer in the company— Charlotte Clemens of Vancouver, Canada. Charlotte earned $65,630 on her own personal sales. However, that was just one third of her total earnings. She had developed a large organization over several summers, so her total earnings came to over $180,000 in just one summer!

Nate had another feather in his cap, another woman. Jessica Tate of Vancouver had the #1 team in the country. Notice that all these high performers were *women*!

I told Nate that my proudest achievement as a sales manager had been to recruit the *first woman student dealer*, Cheryl McElhose of the University of Kansas, back in 1969. Nate told me he was grateful for Cheryl because his top producers every summer are almost always women and 60% of his sales force is composed of women!

> - *Some things never change.*
> - Back in the 60's we motivated everyone to work *13 hours a day* so they could win the Gold Award.
> - That has not changed.
> - It is still the key to success.

In addition, back in the 60's we motivated everyone to make *30 demonstrations a day*. That has not changed either. **Work the hours;**

make the demos. You will succeed. This is the success formula for Southwestern. It is the success formula for your sales career, no matter what business you are in!

The current management structure offers multiple opportunities to students as well as to full-time people out of college.

Title	Units sold
Student Manager	25,000 Independent contractor
Associate Sales Manager	40,000 Employee, sells full time in summer
Field Manager	60,000 Employee, sells full time in summer
District Sales Manager	85,000
Regional Sales Manager	200,000
Regional Sales Director	300,000
Sales Director	500,000
Vice President	750,000
Senior Vice President	1,000,000

Nate is at the Sales Director level, meaning he is responsible for 500,000 units per year. Each unit represents about $13.00 retail, so his organization sells approximately $6,500,000 retail during the 12 weeks of the summer.

Students not only have an opportunity to earn a lot of money during the summer. You learn how to meet and deal with people. You learn how to handle rejection and how to win people's trust. Above all, a student learns self-discipline and personal motivation.

> - I spent six years in college by the time I got my MBA.
> - Four years at Wheaton College and two years at Michigan State University.
> - I have always felt that *I learned more in five summers of selling books than in six years of college!*

http://www.southwestern.com

Savage Sales Secret #21

Be funny without telling jokes

A good salesperson makes good use of humor. However, the intelligent use of humor is *not* what many salespeople think it is.

Here is what it is *not*. It is *not telling jokes*.

Many salespeople turn off their customers by telling them a corny joke. They turn them off even more by telling an off-color joke. Jokes are dangerous. Don't use them, except in rare situations when you are absolutely sure of yourself and have a joke that is short, crisp, clean and proven over and over.

Self-deprecating humor

The best use of humor is when you tell a story that is funny. Usually, the funniest stories are self-deprecating ones—where you put yourself down in a funny way.

Often I give a talk on "driving decisions down" in which I convince managers that they need to "let go" and allow their employees to make decisions. I tell the following story: "Back in the days when my wife Barrie and I were still working out of our garage, before we got into the big leagues, we used to make *all* the decisions. (Pause). Let me modify that. My wife made *most* of the decisions. (Pause). No, no, no. I'm just kidding. She made *all* the decisions!" I pause, and everyone always laughs. Then I go on to tell the story of how we had to let go of our decision-making habits and let others decide.

My father

I have another speech on "making everyone in your company feel important." Here is the story: "My father was an old-time Baptist preacher, a genuine foot-stomping, Bible-thumping, come-to-Jesus preacher. I don't agree with everything he taught.

"For example, I don't think it's a sin to drink a glass of wine. (Pause.)

"I don't think it's a sin to dance. (Wiggle.)

"And I don't think all Catholics are going to Hell!" (Laughter.)

Then I go on to tell the story of how Dad influenced me profoundly by the way he treated everyone with love and respect—and how you should do the same with all your employees.

If I simply told everyone to treat their employees with love and respect, they would yawn and say "Ho hum, we've heard that before." But when I build up to it with a humorous story, including things that I disagree with Dad on, they are ready for the real message.

Zona Rosa, Zona Roja

I always have fun when I make a speech in Spanish. Although my Spanish is almost perfect, thanks to the fact that my parents were missionaries in Ecuador, I can always poke fun at myself and other "gringos" with our foibles with the language.

In Mexico City, one of the most exclusive and posh neighborhoods is called "*La Zona Rosa*" (The Pink Zone). There you will find many exclusive shops, elegant restaurants and fine hotels. Here is my story, usually told in Spanish:

"I was doing a consulting project for Revlon in Mexico City. The marketing manager was Sara González. She asked me to do a marketing study to see how Revlon products were being sold in the Pink Zone (*Zona Rosa*). So, I went to all the department stores, pharmacies and boutiques in the Pink Zone and took careful notes of all the displays, brands, customer reaction and sales presentations. I interviewed sales clerks and asked them how they liked the Revlon brands compared to the other brands they were selling.

"The next day I went back to see Sara at Revlon headquarters. I reported, 'Sara, I did just what you asked me to do. Last night I went to the *Zona Roja* (Red Zone).'"

Sara gasped and blurted out, horrified, "Steve, I never asked you to go the Red Zone! (*Zona Roja*) I asked you to go to the Pink Zone! (*Zona Rosa*)" (The "red zone" is where the prostitutes hang out!)

Everyone laughs.

Thus, you make your audience laugh with self-deprecating humor. By putting yourself down, they like you better. Whether you tell this story to one person or 500 people, it works like a charm.

Savage Sales Secret #22

Use "random facts" to get in and make friends

Golden nugget sales secrets

Rory Vaden is famous for being the leader of the "*Take the Stairs World Tour.*" It's a social movement where thousands of people from dozens of countries commit to *take the stairs* more often as a physical reminder of their commitment to be more disciplined and to do the hard work it takes to be successful in life. Rory has appeared on Oprah Radio with Dr. Oz and is often invited to speak in the media and at company events sharing insights about leveraging discipline to get better results.

One technique I discovered from Rory about selling in a one-on-one situation is something he calls using *golden nuggets*.

On the pre-approach, for example, Rory likes to get as much information as fast as he can. A *golden nugget* is a random fact about the prospect that most salespeople would ignore—but that Rory uses to establish immediate rapport. When Rory was a college student selling books for Southwestern Company, he would ask, "Does the family across the street have kids in school? How do you know them?"

"Their dog, Coco, comes over here a lot."

Bingo! Rory has a *golden nugget*.

He dashes across the street, knocks on the door and waits. The woman answers the door, hesitantly, cautiously. Rory says, "Hi, I'm Rory. I'm calling on folks whose kids go to Franklin Elementary School and have dogs named Coco."

The ice is broken. The woman laughs, opens the door and lets Rory come in.

That was back in college. Now Rory is a public speaker, doing keynotes and seminars. After he does a seminar, he asks the seminar organizer for referrals. Rory asks, "Is there anybody else like you in a different city?"

"Yes. I know Joe Jones with XYZ Electronics."

"How did you get to know Joe?"

"Oh, we were in an event together in Las Vegas. We stayed up until 4 AM one morning drinking beer. He's a character."

Bingo! Rory has a *golden nugget*. He calls Joe Jones and says, "Carl Anderson from ABC Electronics asked me to give you a call. He says you guys had a crazy time in Las Vegas at the last convention."

Joe is immediately loose and relaxed. Rory can now go on and talk about his seminars.

Dealing with gate keepers

Rory has some great lines to use with *"gate keepers"* –secretaries and assistants who block the way from getting you to talk with the decision-maker. (In an earlier chapter, I referred to them as *"guard dogs."* Same thing.) Rory has identified four "death questions" that gate keepers ask:

The four "death questions:"

1. Whom may I say is calling?
2. What is this call regarding?
3. Is he expecting your call?
4. What company are you with?

Rory says, "Answering any of these questions brings you closer to the death of your sale. Secretaries are 100% trained to screen you and send you to *voice jail.*"

"OK, Rory, so how do you handle those four death questions?"

"There are two ways to do it. First of all, you can avoid the secretary altogether by calling a salesperson. Often I ask to be transferred to the sales side of the company. The receptionist is always happy to do that. Once I get a salesperson on the phone, they are always happy to talk and share information. Often the salesperson will transfer me directly to the decision-maker.

"The second way is to answer the *death question* by being confident and bold and saying one of the following:

1. "You can let him know it's regarding Rory Vaden.
2. "I'm sure if you mention Rory Vaden, it will be fine, thank you."

Remembering names

Rory is a master at remembering names. He says that most companies don't sort prospect lists properly. He tries to get items that are non-business related into his data base, like clubs and special interests. Then, when he meets someone, he will mention, "Gary Jones mentioned to me that you play golf together every weekend. He said you almost always beat him by 3 or 4 holes." While Rory is saying this, he is looking at the person's face and thinking "golf and Gary." The association helps this person's face and name become indelibly inscribed in Rory's mind. Rory has accomplished two things in one sentence:

1. He has gotten the person relaxed by talking about his golf with his buddy.
2. He has taken the first step towards remembering his name.

I have seen Rory meet a group of 15 or 20 people and then make a group presentation. During his presentation, he addresses each person in the group by name. The audience is amazed and stunned. They warm up to Rory and buy whatever he is offering, whether it is a keynote speech, tickets to a seminar or a consulting project. I thought I was good at remembering names, but Rory's performance was light years ahead of anything I had ever done. I asked him how he did it. He then told me how he had developed seven "tions" of remembering people's names.

Relaxation—the number one reason we forget a name is because we are stressed out or thinking about something else.

Repetition—Repeat someone's name to yourself at least 3 to 5 times in the first 15 seconds to program it into your memory.

Utilization—Use someone's name when you're talking to them, especially right when you first meet them. (Example: "Hey, Joe....Joe last name? Nice to meet you, Joe. Joe, where are you from?)

Association—Make their first name rhyme with something or create an alliterative pattern. (Example: "Hannah banana" or "Angela Apple.")

Recognition—Overlay a new person's face with the face of someone you know extremely well. (Example: my brother's name is Bobby so any time I meet someone named Bobby I mentally connect them with my brother whom I will never forget.)

Picturization—Remember pictures are the language of the mind. Many names are automatically pictures that you can associate with a picture. (Examples—Robin, Reed, Holly, Bob, Matt, etc.)

Finalization—It is crucial to end every conversation by using the person's name so that it is one of the last things on your mind.

Rory's ideas are fantastic and I have remembered a lot more names since I started using them.

I would like to add one of my own techniques while we are on the subject. When I meet a new person, I picture his or her name blazing in screaming Day-Glo paint on their forehead. The color violet works well for me. Thus, I'd like to take the freedom to add an eighth "tion" to Rory's list and call it "***blazification***."

Introduction sales secrets

Rory has gone from pre-approach to approach. Now he is ready for the *introduction* phase of his sales process. This is where he figures out what the customer needs and wants. He never jumps into his presentation without paving the way. Many salespeople make the mistake of starting their sales pitch too quickly. Yakkity yakkity yak. The customer gets bored. Sale is lost.

Rory's philosophy is to *listen way more than to talk*. That way he finds out all the reasons to sell them. He says there are basically three ways to get a person to do something:

1. Force them to do it with guns, threats or commands.
2. Ask them to do it.
3. Get them to realize the benefits that are in it for themselves.

Rory always aims for Option #3. He thinks of it as a line of Socratic inquiry, by which he asks a series of questions, guiding the customer to the realization that this is the product that will fulfill their needs.

Presentation sales secrets

Rory feels that a good introduction makes a presentation almost an afterthought. In his presentation he uses humor and tailors it to the individual. At this point, while he is describing the features of his product, he will probably be talking more than the customer.

Closing sales secrets

Rory memorizes his close word-for-word. It is a formality, almost like a green light. You ask a series of questions. If the customer said "yes" to each one, then the close is simply another green light.

Here are some of the incremental green lights Rory got when he was selling books with Southwestern:

"If you were able to wait and save up for the books between now and September, would that make it easier?" ("Yes." Green light.)

"I will mail you a postcard a week before I deliver your books. Do you use your home address or a PO Box?" ("Home address." Green light.)

"I'll stop by to deliver your books during the last week of August. Will you be home that week or on vacation?" ("I'll be home." Green light.)

"OK, I'll see you in August. Most people like to pay part of it now and the rest in August. Some folks pay half, others pay a third. What would be most convenient for you?" ("I'll pay a third." Green light. Sale complete.)

Notice that Rory never asks, "Do you want to buy these books?" That would be a *yes* or *no* question. Instead, he asks a series of gentle, easy, non-threatening questions that wind up leading to a sale.

Rory has written a great book on humor called **No Laughs to Know Laughs**. The subtitle is "How to Be Funny to Make More Money!" It is a great tool for anyone in sales or public speaking.

Rory is one of three partners, along with Dustin Hillis and Gary Michels, in Success Starts Now!™ They have built a marvelous company that conducts phenomenal and productive sales seminars, followed up by high-value coaching.

Their website is www.ssnseminars.com.

Rory also has his own website: www.roryvaden.com.

Savage Sales Secret #23

Get new business through referrals

Once you do a good job for someone, you should immediately ask that person for the names of three other people that you should call. When you call those people, you have a huge head start. You start out saying, "Hi, I'm Steve Savage. Charlie Johnson used me to help him fire up his sales force. His sales increased 16% in the past 6 months. He thought you and I ought to get acquainted. I'm going to be in your area tomorrow afternoon and was wondering if I could stop by for 5 minutes to say hello. Are you available at 2 PM or would 4 PM be better?"

Most of the people with whom I have done business have come through referrals. When we bought our 200-acre farm in Vermont, our real estate agent, Jan, referred us to our contractor and our interior decorator. Ron, the contractor, had established a reputation as the best person in the area for restoring old Vermont farm homes. I never would have known about him if Jan had not referred him. But he had done his due diligence for years, getting to know all the real estate agents in town, giving them his business card and literature. When we needed to restore our 1791 Vermont farmhouse, Jan told us to call Ron.

When Ron was done with his work, he referred us to Betty, the interior designer. She was the best in the area. She had done the same thing as Ron—given out her business card and literature to all the contractors in the area. Thus, there was a network of people that knew each other and referred each other.

You need to constantly promote yourself whenever you go to meetings, the bank, cocktail parties or any business luncheon. Don't be shy. My friend Patricia Fripp, the famous speaker, calls it *"shameless self-promotion."* She promotes herself constantly. She has encouraged me and others she has trained to promote themselves as well.

Savage Sales Secret #24

Give your customer unexpected and free bonus value

Wedding rings

I have bought my wife Barrie two wedding rings. The first was when I was nearly bankrupt. The second was after I had sold my company to Colgate-Palmolive. Both rings are treasures. Both rings were sold to us by master salespeople. Each salesperson was entirely different.

When I proposed to Barrie in 1976, our company was in the process of shutting down. We had failed. The sad and dramatic story is told in my book **Guerrilla Business Secrets**. I had almost no money but was already starting a new business. The comforting part of my marriage proposal was this: when she said "yes" I knew she was not marrying me for my money!

We were living in California. We went to the little town of Marshall, near Tomales Bay, north of San Francisco. We had visited Point Reyes National Seashore and stumbled into a goldsmith's shop. His name was Glenn. We watched him work and looked at some of his creations. We loved his designs, mostly necklaces and bracelets. Then we noticed some rings. We asked Glenn if he could custom design two wedding rings.

"Yes," he replied, "that's my specialty."

It was the 70's and Glenn was your classic hippie. He was definitely not your standard salesperson. But through his sincerity and honesty, we were convinced he was the guy we wanted for our wedding rings. He described the process he would use. He would carve a design into a piece of charcoal. The design would be patterned after a leaf. Then he would cast both rings in the same design. What a great idea!

The price was amazingly low. Even though we were starting over, we could afford it. We put him to work. A few days later, the job was done. The rings were superb works of art, exquisite craftsmanship, a special and unique bond for Barrie and me. We have worn them for 38 years.

The diamond ring

Ten years later we had sold our company to Colgate Palmolive. It was time to buy Barrie her first diamond ring. We now lived in Vermont. I went to Nick, our local jeweler, and told him what I wanted. He showed me some jewelry he had recently purchased in an estate sale. He pulled out an elegant diamond, dazzling and pure. He did not have to sell me. I said, "Yes."

I wanted a simple setting so the diamond could show forth its facets. Nick gave me exactly what I wanted. It was dazzling and lustrous.

When I gave it to Barrie, it was with joy and pride. She looked stunning with her stylish and well-designed diamond. However, she still loved her original gold ring and often wore the two together.

Nick's salesmanship was continual. Every time he saw Barrie go into his store, he would greet her and offer to clean the diamond. He wanted it to sparkle and glitter. A couple of times, he met her on the streets of our small town. He would always look at her hand and say, "Please come in the shop and let me clean your ring!" This is first-class salesmanship at its best!

Savage Sales Secret #25

Recruit top people

The Southwestern Company always has a wealth of highly trained college graduates every year who have spent several summers selling books door-to-door. Many years ago they set up a Placement Office to help students find a good sales job after graduation. At first, the Placement Office was devoted primarily to helping students get jobs with other Southwestern-related companies, especially Tom James Company and Great American Opportunities.

That all changed in 1982 when Carl Roberts took over the Placement Office. At first, his main job was to counsel 300 to 400 graduating seniors and MBA students, advising them on their career choices or helping them get into graduate or a professional school.

Carl had sold books for six summers and knew what a gold mine he had on his hands. He quickly realized that many of the Southwestern students were excellent candidates for hundreds of companies all across America. He hired Greg Boucher, a Southwestern Alumni, to help him tap this vast market. Together, they started lining up other companies to use their services.

Greg and Carl used the good old Southwestern "pre-approach" technique—find someone who already knows and likes you who can get you in the door. They called Matthew Bender, a company that sold legal books to attorneys. There was already a Southwestern Alumnus working there, proving that experience selling books was a sure-fire guarantee of success.

Carl said, "How would you like to have a steady stream of salespeople each year, just like Joe?"

"Yes, of course. How do we get them?"

The match was made. Carl negotiated an employer-based fee and Matthew Bender quickly became one of the first big clients.

The Placement Office had been set up as a service to the college students and as a recruiting tool for other Southwestern subsidiaries. Now, suddenly, Carl and Greg found that they had a genuine "guerrilla" business opportunity. This was not merely a "Placement Office." This was a *company that could generate a profit and be scalable*!

I asked Carl to expand on his concept of "scalable."

"To me, *scalable* means you have built a model that can be repeated. We have a unique way of doing business but we can teach it to other people. We can repeat our formula. Thus, we can bring new recruiters into our company, teach them our philosophy, our values and our approach to recruiting. That is *scalable*. A *non-scalable* business would be one in which the idea of the founder was so unique that it could not be repeated. We have been able to grow on a solid foundation that is sustainable and repeatable.

An "intrapreneurial company"

They named the company SBR—Southwestern Business Resources. Carl dubbed it an "*intrapreneurial company*." He said, "I was starting a business within a business. We had the Southwestern infrastructure to help us. Most entrepreneurs spend 40% to 50% of their time on non-selling aspects such as taxes and accounting. Young companies have to struggle. They don't have a safety net."

Carl elaborated. "Southwestern people like selling. They like building teams. Here at SBR we can focus on our strengths, not our weaknesses. We can focus on stuff we are good at."

This made me think of the way the entire "Guerrilla Marketing" theme had evolved since 1983. I told Carl, "When Jay Levinson wrote his first edition of **Guerrilla Marketing** back in 1983, he thought his market was going to be small to medium-sized businesses. I was one of his original "guerrillas" and he used our company out in California as one of his models for a classic guerrilla company. Since then, Jay has discovered that a lot of large companies have bought the book and have sent their marketing people to his seminars. In fact, I do a lot of Guerrilla Marketing seminars in Spanish in Latin America. About half my audience usually consists of sales managers and marketing managers from large companies. They realize that they have to adapt guerrilla tactics in order to compete against the small companies or else the guerrillas will eat them alive.

"I commend you, Carl, because you recognized this way back in 1983 and 1984, when Jay was first launching his Guerrilla Marketing books. You took a concept that was just gathering steam back in the 1980's: *intrapreneurial!* I love that word! It really captures the essence of a large company setting up a small business within its corporate structure and setting the leaders of the company free to operate it without all kinds of corporate rules and bureaucracy. Congratulations!"

As we chatted, I was still assuming that SBR was placing salespeople in companies across America. Carl suddenly changed my thinking. He said, "Yes, Steve, we used to place *salespeople* and that's all we did. But then we started getting requests for accountants, computer technicians, health care professionals and biotech scientists. We have even developed a special relationship with the Defense Industry in which we supply them with people skilled in artificial intelligence security cleared professionals!

"We work just as hard on these careers as on the salespeople. In fact, many of the Southwestern Alumni go into fields other than sales. We are recruiting people in the manufacturing, nonprofit, consumer goods, banking, equipment leasing, software and real estate industries. And I'm not just talking about real estate sales. We take care of all the key jobs from project manager to property manager."

I asked, "Carl, what percentage of your recruits are Southwestern Alumni?"

"You'll be surprised, Steve, but only 5% are Southwestern Alumni. The rest are from all over the world. Southwestern allowed us to grow and formed our foundation. The core Southwestern values form our culture and philosophy. Those values allow our company to grow around a common set of principles."

My next question was a bit skeptical. "Carl, why does a company need you? Why would they pay you a big fee when they could just run some ads and recruit people directly?"

This came right to the heart of the matter. In fact, this is the essence of any great salesmanship. *You must fulfill a need.* Here is the need filled by SBR Recruiting:

"What happens," Carl replied, "is that Human Resources departments get bogged down in paperwork. They get hundreds of resumes. It's overwhelming.

"Our presentation to an HR Department is quite simple. Let's say you are the HR Manager of a major corporation. I would say to you, 'Steve, we take a targeted rifle approach. Tell us what skill sets you need. We will extract that talent you need.'"

I asked Carl, "What if they tell you they can run an ad in the paper?"

Carl laughed. "I love that one. I just ask them, 'When was the last time you read a classified ad?' They always smile and shake their heads. Then I follow up with, 'Well, Arlene, if *you* don't read a classified, why do you want to hire someone who spends hours every Sunday looking at classifieds?'"

Carl told me that SBR had grown over the years and they now have 45 full-time recruiters. Most of them specialize in specific industries and become known for their expertise and ability to get the right person for the right job.

Commission structure sales secrets

I asked Carl how he motivates his recruiters.

"We always try to analyze how we can be different from our competition. Many recruitment firms pay straight commission. We pay our recruiters a base plus commission and benefits. In addition they have a chance to get an equity position in the company. We are fortunate that Spencer Hays years ago initiated a program that allowed employees to have an equity position in the company. This encourages all of us to watch the profits and grow the company because we directly benefit. In essence, our recruiters get a better structure, training and support than they would get with other recruiting companies."

Carl shared with me the SBR Company Philosophies which were given to him by Spencer Hays, Executive Chairman of Southwestern, the parent company of SBR. I recommend that you study these 20 philosophies carefully. Read them over and over. Apply them to your own business and you will find your company culture changing to a positive and energetic environment. The natural result of this is that you will find your sales growing, along with your profits!

Company philosophy sales secrets

1. We believe in excellence and make it a habit.
2. We strongly believe that we cannot build a business; we build people, and people build the business. We put great emphasis on creating an atmosphere in which people can take their God-given talents, skills and capabilities and have fun achieving and accomplishing.
3. We strongly believe that we are in business to serve our customers, and the way to maintain customers is to always give more value than we charge for.
4. We strongly believe that management's first responsibility is to run the company in such a way that it makes money. If not, how can the company stay in business and continue giving customers the good quality products they want?
5. We strongly believe it is management's responsibility to guarantee every worker in our business job security, and the only way we can do that is to run the company in such a way that we make money. The only way a company can make money is to grow its sales. If a company's sales stay the same, with expenses going up every year, it makes less money. The only way a company can grow its profits is to grow its sales.

6. We strongly believe in taking from profit each year and putting that back into the business, enabling us to give even better products and services to our customers.

7. We have a profit-sharing plan as part of our business. We believe it is our responsibility to give each employee the opportunity to retire with dignity and self-respect.

8. All of the key people within our companies own part of the business. They have an owner's viewpoint and perspective. Therefore, they will always give the very best quality and service and remember that the customer is first.

9. Waste leads to want, so we work very hard not to squander money. This means we have more money to spend on better services and products for our customers.

10. We believe in the importance of a wholesome and good attitude. If we think we can, we can. We can, we will, we are going to excel and succeed.

11. Never be part of the problem; be part of the solution to the problem. People like this are motivational and inspiring to others.

12. Little people get upset over little things; big people don't. Unfortunately, a lot of people go through their entire lives getting upset and spending a lot of time and energy on incidental things that don't make a bit of difference.

13. Form the habit of doing things failures don't like to do. Failures don't like to plan in advance. They don't like to call and make their appointments in advance. They don't like to see a certain number of new people each day. They don't like to confront people about actions that are not consistent with their goals.

14. We live in an age of intellectual giants and emotional midgets. We can put a man on the moon and bring him back, but we can't control ourselves and overcome our emotions enough to overcome the fear of failure and the fear of rejection. Many times we are so afraid we can't do something that we don't even attempt it.

15. The way to overcome the fear of rejection is to make the call! The way to overcome the fear of failure is to keep figuring out better and better ways of doing our job. If we don't succeed at first, keep trying and trying.

16. There is no limit to what can be accomplished, if we are not hung up on who gets the credit.

17. Set high goals, give good self-talk and be accountable.

18. What we are someday going to be, we are now becoming.

19. We are all part of a team. It takes many people doing many different things to build a great company—no one can do it alone.

20. Real success is doing our best.

Carl told me, "These twenty philosophies are part of the fabric of the Southwestern family of companies. We don't just give them lip service. They motivate us in a fundamental way."

"Carl," I replied, "I have lived by these principles ever since I sold books with Southwestern back in college. It is refreshing to hear them stated again. But now let's get down to the nitty-gritty. Tell me about the nuts and bolts of getting a company to use your services to recruit for them. Your recruiters are basically salespeople. They have to sell a company on using you. Then they have to find the right candidate and sell that person on joining the company!"

"Yes, there are many different aspects to obtaining a search assignment, otherwise known as a job order, and recruiting a top candidate. Rather than focusing on our specific approaches, let me tell you some key principles that apply to many sales situations. When our recruiters follow these principles they are successful, regardless of what presentation they use."

"Great! That will help every reader of this book!"

"First, *use several types of media*—live call, voice mail, email, fax, old-fashioned mail, blogs, social networks, Twitter, etc. We have found that most people have a preferred way of communicating. It is the salesperson's job to figure it out for each client.

"Second, *make lots of calls*. I had a recruiter once who made seventeen calls to the hiring authority before he succeeded in speaking with the person. We ended up doing multiple searches for him. He turned out to be a great client even though we initially had a hard time connecting.

"Third, *ask questions and listen*. The best salespeople will question their way to a sale rather than talk their way to one. Many times we try to control a conversation by talking. I have found it more fun, interesting and challenging to use questions to control and direct a conversation."

I interrupted. "Yes! That is one my passions. I always teach my salespeople to ask tons of questions and make sure the customer does at least 50% of the talking! OK, Carl, you've covered three of your sales principles. What else?"

"Here's the fourth. *Network*. Our best salespeople/recruiters are terrific networkers. They gather information from others and then use it and their contacts to move the ball down the field.

"Fifth, *do your homework*. In today's world, it is so easy to know your client's goals, mission and culture, that you should never go into a call or presentation flying by the seat of your pants. Our best consultants go in prepared, and the feedback is so much more positive. If you are unprepared, you make the client think you are not interested and not committed to doing your best. So take a little time and plan ahead. This is why our domain name is www.thinkingahead.com. We want to be out in front and plan for all contingencies.

Sixth, *feed your mind*. There are many books, tapes, CD's and DVD's to help you. Find the style and content that works for you. Then pursue it with diligence.

Finally, *work your plan*. Do it every day. In the book business we learned it takes twenty-one days to form a good habit and only one break it! Be conscientious and committed to working each day as if it were your last."

How to sell yourself all the way to a PhD degree!

Carl Roberts has a PhD in Public Health and Biostatistics. I was intrigued with how he got his PhD and why he eventually became president of a company instead of professor at a university. His story is a great example of salesmanship and persistence and belongs as a classic in "*Savage Sales Secrets.*"

"Well, Steve, it wasn't easy. I found out there are a lot of brilliant people in grad schools who have earned their "ABD."

"What's the *ABD*?" I asked.

Carl grinned. "*All but the dissertation*! Well, I had spent six summers knocking on doors. The main thing I learned was that if I persist, I can do it.

"My doctoral committee turned down my first chapter **30 times**! But, they had never dealt with a book salesperson! I knew they would never wear me out. The persistence I learned selling books got me my PhD. I don't have incredible sales talent. But I do have bulldog persistence."

Carl's story will inspire you no matter what line of sales you are in. Remember, no matter how many times you get rejected, Carl got rejected 30 times before his dissertation was accepted. And remember that Carl has gone on to become a hugely successful "*intrapreneur*" leading a company whose sales are growing at an annual rate of over 30%.

- Carl's personal "sales secret" to getting a PhD:
- *Bulldog persistence!*

---

www.thinkingahead.com

Savage Sales Secret #26

Sell sophisticated products "soft and easy"

What is the picture in your mind of a person who sells investments? Yes, you are probably imagining a tense, harried, high-pressure Harvard MBA working in an investment office in Manhattan, pounding the phones, popping anti-ulcer pills and making a fortune.

But picture this instead. A genuine, relaxed human being goes out and actually *knocks on doors*, low-keyed, casual and easy. That's right, the man or woman who is an investment advisor with Southwestern Investments gets established in the community simply by knocking on doors and making friends.

Study the following approach, presentation and close. Picture in your own mind how you can adapt these low-keyed yet powerful techniques to your own business. Here's how it goes:

"Hi, are you Mark Deering? Great! My name is Luke Aull. I own a small business here in the neighborhood and today I am out doing some advertising the old fashioned way.

"Tell me. How long have you lived here in the area? What kind of changes have you seen? What brought you here?

"Is there a special reason I caught you at home today?

If the reply is, "I work," you say, "Great! What do you do for a living? How did you get into that business?

If the reply is, "I'm retired," you say, "Great! What kinds of things do you do to keep yourself occupied?

"I promised I wouldn't take up too much time. I am a financial planner with Southwestern Investment Services. My office is…well, are you familiar with the Southwestern Company, located off Atrium Way?

"Do you ever get to listen to Dave Ramsey on the radio? We're his endorsed local provider. That's something we're pretty proud of. He saw that we were honest and ethical with our clients.

"Tell me. What's been your favorite investment over the last five years?"

If they say "401K," you say, "Great! What types of things do you invest in your 401K? How do you make investment decisions inside your plan? When was the last time you had a professional review your plan for you?

"From time to time we have some interesting seminars on investing, taxes and retirement planning. I'd like to drop you an invitation in the mail. When I see something of interest, what is the best way to send it to you? When I mail or email out that invitation, what is the best phone number to reach you to confirm that you received it?

"What would a real-life perfect investment look like to you?" (They answer.) Typically, their answer is out of the ballpark, so you have to reset the boundaries. The best way is to use humor. "Ha! I don't know if I can find something paying 100% per year, but if I run across something up to those standards, I will be sure to let you know!"

What do you think of this approach? Did you ever imagine selling investments in such a "soft" and friendly manner? Do you see why it works? Can you think of ways to apply these *"sales secrets"* to your own business?

Let's go behind the scenes now and get acquainted with this unusual investment company.

By now you are aware that I am fascinated with the Southwestern Company where I learned about selling when I was a 19-year-old college student. Several of my examples in this book come from Southwestern. The company started as a publishing company over 150 years ago, but in the last 20-30 years it has mushroomed into a great variety of companies, each with its own unique flavor, but each grounded in a similar philosophy and values.

Jeff Dobyns (pronounced Doe-bines) has been president of Southwestern Investments since 2002. However, back in the 1990's, he cut his teeth selling books door-to-door during four summers. He attended Ohio University in Athens, Ohio, majoring in finance.

When he graduated, Jeff wanted to start his own business. His friend, Ron Lykins, was a CPA. There was a big trend in the mid-90's for CPA's to get into the investment business. However, most CPA's were not very good at selling! Ron saw a great opportunity with Jeff: a finance major with sales experience!

Jeff plunged in. He took advantage of Ron's vast background in taxes and finance. Ron took advantage of Jeff's incredible experience in sales. And they took off! Within three years, Jeff's investment group was pulling in more revenue than Ron's traditional tax business with six CPA's!

Jeff said, "I could not have done it alone. Ron had the structure in place. I could focus on my strength: selling.

In 2002, the Southwestern Company talked to Jeff about setting up an investment company under the Southwestern "umbrella." Southwestern had already done some insurance sales under one of their other divisions. However, they wanted a company to specialize just in investments. Jeff was excited, because he saw the possibility of expanding all the knowledge he had gained into something much bigger. He moved to Nashville and launched the investments business.

Similar to SBR Recruiters, this was a perfect *intrapreneurial* situation. The Southwestern Company provided its building with office space as well as personnel to help with logistics. The corporate structure was set. Jeff was free to do what he loved, and what he did best: ***sell***.

To start with credibility, Jeff hooked his fledgling investment company up with the established firm, Raymond James Investments. Thus, from the outset, Southwestern Investments could offer the same investment advice as any investment company. Raymond James was considered the #1 business model for successful brokers who left brokerage firms and wanted to start their own companies. It was an ideal relationship for Jeff and Southwestern. The business was launched.

The strategic alliance model

Jeff used another *"sales secret"* by establishing a relationship with the well-known radio financial talk show host, Dave Ramsey. He proved himself with Dave Ramsey in Brentwood, Tennessee, a suburb south of Nashville. Going door-to-door as well as business-to-business, Jeff proved to Dave Ramsey that the Southwestern Investments model was sound, ethical, conservative and profitable. Dave announced on his radio show that Jeff and his team were now an ELP (Established Local Provider) in Franklin, Tennessee.

This was a huge thrust upward. In each town where Southwestern Investments had financial planners, they dedicated themselves to proving that they deserved the ELP designation. Listeners to Ramsey's popular program signed up. Ramsey himself entrusted his company's retirement plan to Jeff and Southwestern Investments.

I asked Jeff if they had tried telemarketing. "Yes, we have," he replied, "but it is not as effective for us as cold calling. We have a much higher penetration rate if we call on homes or offices. This is our formula for success."

"How would you define your business model?"

"We have three guiding principles that have guided us and made us successful," said Jeff.

- "We take good care of our customers.
- "We are not pushy.
- "We are comprehensive."

Apply those three *sales secrets* to your business and you will run a clean, solid, respected and profitable business.

Client rights sales secrets

Jeff publishes nine "rights" that each client can expect. These rights are published right on the home page of SWI's website. Each client gets a copy of these rights during the very first visit.

Your Rights as a Client:

- Courteous Service
- A Trustworthy and Competent Financial Advisor
- Suitable Recommendations
- Timely Transactions at the Best Available Prices
- Full Disclosure of Costs and Risks
- Clear Communications
- Comprehensive Statements and Trade Confirmations
- Prompt Error and Complaint Resolution
- Strict Confidentiality

Armed with these "rights," a Southwestern Investments Financial Planner can go into any office or any home with pride and self-confidence.

Likewise, you should analyze your own business and develop a set of guiding principles that will define you and give you a mission to fulfill when you go to meet your clients.

I asked Jeff about the difference in technique between calling on a business versus calling on a home.

"When we go to a business, we often set it up a day in advance with the manager. We want to get all the key people in the office at our meeting. We want to manage all of their investment portfolios. Once we have gotten the manager's interest, we come in the next day with donuts and coffee. That gets everyone relaxed. Then we make our presentation."

"What specifically do you say to the manager to convince him or her to let you have a meeting with his people?"

"We make it very low keyed and easy. First, we tell the manager pretty much the same things we tell a person at home. Then we say, 'Joe, most managers ask us to give all their key people a chance to let us become their financial planners. Dave Smith over at XYZ Company had me talk to his managers. Do you know him? OK. All we need is about 15 minutes. I'll bring donuts. What time do you get here in the morning? Would tomorrow be a convenient time or would Thursday be better?'"

Next, I asked Jeff to describe the actual sales presentation and close.

"Normally, we do it in two meetings. The first meeting is to build rapport and to discover the client's goals and objectives. We ask a lot of questions. We also differentiate ourselves from Merrill Lynch, Morgan Stanley and the other well-known investment firms."

"How do you do that?"

"I mention that Merrill Lynch and similar firms often sell their own funds to the client. We are independent. These are not our own investments, so we don't have that inherent conflict of interest. We don't make quite as much money per client, but that's OK, because we build trust."

"How do you make your money?"

"One of two ways. First, we have a fee structure, based on the percentage of money we manage. Second, we earn a commission from the mutual fund. The client can choose."

"How do you get them to trust you?"

"Often, we are there because of a referral, so there is already some trust. But if we are starting cold, we tell them there are 20,000 mutual funds, each with its own internal operating expenses. They have a non-negotiable fee no matter who you're working with. There is no extra cost to working with an independent financial planner. When you are independent, you can recommend what's best for your client."

"What if a client has a mutual fund he is excited about?"

"That's perfect for us," replied Jeff. "Most mutual fund salespeople would get into a combative debate. In our case, we say we don't care what you use. We want you to use funds that will meet a series of criteria. We don't debate that fund. We just establish a philosophy."

"Sounds like you still have the good old Southwestern a[...] asking a lot of questions and letting the client do a lot of tal[...]

"Yes! That is really the best way to take control of the meeting. Then you have a productive meeting and people relax. They know they won't get sold and pressured. They just give us data."

"How do you close the sale?"

"That's usually on the second meeting. If we do everything right, the close is natural. We come back with an action list. We tell the client, 'Here are the things we need to do.' Then we give them six to twelve action items—all things that are beneficial to the client. At the end we simply say, "OK! We've got all the paperwork. What are the highest priorities for you?"

"Sounds great. What is your closing rate?"

"90%."

"Wow!"

Referral sales secrets

Southwestern Investments has a great way of getting referrals. They have grown their business dramatically with little fanfare simply by intelligently using referrals. Here is the way they tell their investment advisers how to do it:

Gathering referrals is perhaps the most efficient way to grow your business. Referrals do not cost you anything to ask for, they take very little extra time to ask for and they are much stronger prospects because they know someone you already have a relationship with. Once you start asking for them they become a self-perpetuating prospecting system.

The key to getting referrals is to just ask for them. The following is a referral sales talk:

"Mr. Smith, I sure have enjoyed visiting with you today. Before I go, I wanted to ask a quick favor of you.

"I have focused on building my client base through referrals. I have found this to be the most efficient system for my clients and myself. Most everyone I talk to knows a couple of people that may not be happy with the current financial help they are getting, or may be getting ready to retire and do not have a relationship with someone who can help them take care of their retirement, or may just have a couple of simple questions, but do not know who to ask.

"I am a pretty low-key person, and typically just call referrals and introduce myself. Let me ask you, who are family members you have here in the area that I should give a call to? (Keep asking until they run out of family members.) Who are a few people with whom you go to church? (Keep asking until they run out.) Who are a few people you work with? (Keep asking until they run out.) Anyone you went to school with? (Keep asking until they run out.)

When asking for referrals, first get all the names. Once you have gotten all the names, go back and get all their phone numbers, and perhaps where they live. Once you have gotten their contact info go back and find out their relation to the person who referred them. Use a set form on which to write this information.

- Using referrals as a part of your client building plan will generate terrific long-term results. Just do it!

Follow-up letter sales secrets

A successful salesperson always follows up with a letter, a postcard or a phone call. Jeff has created a series of letters to follow up with each customer. The letters are short, business-like and friendly. Use this as a model for your own business and make sure you follow up every time you make a sale.

Month, 1, 200x

Name
Address
City, ST Zip

Dear Salutation:

It was a real pleasure speaking with you as we discussed your financial situation.

Enclosed, please find the necessary paperwork to transfer your IRA. Please complete the highlighted sections, sign the forms where I have indicated, and return to me in the enclosed envelope along with a copy of a statement from your current account.

Thank you again for the opportunity to earn your business. I look forward to a long, productive relationship in helping you achieve all of your financial goals safely and comfortably. If you have any questions, please feel free to call me at XXX-XXXX.

Sincerely,

Jeffrey T. Dobyns, CFP*, CLU, ChFC
President-Southwestern Investment Services, Inc.

Surviving and thriving in tough economic times

In the last six months of 2008, while the United States and the entire world were slipping into a severe recession, Southwestern Investments increased their sales by 45% over the last six months of 2007. Each financial planner increased his or her own personal sales by 20% to 80% over 2007. This was during the stock market crash, the housing crash and every other panic that was going on. Jeff and his team of 19 financial planners proved the famous Robert Schuller saying: "Tough times never last but tough people do."

You can also survive tough economic times by following the same principles that have guided Jeff and his team of financial planners.

> • Absorb the lessons of this unique investment company and adapt them to your own business.
> • You will survive and *thrive* in good times and bad.

www.raymondjames.com/southwestern

Savage Sales Secret #27

Sell through low-keyed honesty

Health insurance sales have long been stuck in old patterns and time-worn philosophies. The *Savage Sales Secrets* model searches for new ways of selling traditional products. Aflac has won my award as the genuine "*Savage*" in the health insurance industry. Back in 1955, three brothers decided they could go up against the big boys by offering something different—that fulfilled a need left out by traditional health insurance sales.

What was the big gap?

"Out-of-pocket expenses."

Yes, that was the gap seen by the three Amos brothers back in 1955. The big insurance companies covered hospital and doctor bills, but they did not realize that everyone who had an extended hospital stay had major "out-of-pocket" expenses. When you have cancer, you still have to pay your utility bill, house payment, rent, car payment and put food on the table. What are you going to do?

Aflac was set up to take care of that. Their first products in 1955 were cancer and intensive care insurance. When they sold "cancer" insurance, a person was assured that their out-of-pocket expenses were taken care of. Traditional health insurance would help take care of some of the doctor and hospital bills. But Aflac would pay you cash to help take care of the co-payments, deductibles, gas, utilities and other expenses that go on when you are in the hospital.

The main difference between Aflac and traditional health insurance is that Aflac pays cash directly to the policy holder. The person who is insured can use the money for anything. They can spend it as they want.

Patrick Fuller is an Aflac Regional Sales Coordinator in Michigan. He told me that his mother had major medical health insurance. When she had a stroke, major medical paid most of the medical bills. But there were still staggering bills confronting her; home health care costs, costs associated with making her home handicapped accessible, gas expenses to and from the doctors 35 miles away and other incidental expenses. Her Aflac policy helped pay those bills.

My brother, Jim Savage, works with Pat Fuller in Michigan selling Aflac. He is a genuine Savage using *Savage Sales Secrets* to call on businesses in Central Michigan, telling their employees the Aflac story. When Jim approaches an employer, his main goal is to present the Aflac program to the employees. In addition, he wants the employer to agree to deduct the premiums from the payroll.

This is his typical approach to an employer:

"Hi George. I'm Jim Savage. Joe Anderson over at Anderson Machinery said that you guys play golf together every Saturday. I'm their Aflac Rep, and he thought you might be interested in checking out our program. I'm also the Aflac guy for Dr. McKinley's office down on the corner. Do you know Dan McKinley? He sure is a character, isn't he?!

"Has anybody ever told you about Aflac? What both Joe and Dan especially like about it is that it doesn't cost you anything as an employer. Your employees just choose which of our policies make the most sense to them and those policies are then payroll-deducted. They appreciate getting a good group rate for being part of your company.

"What most guys like yourself like to have me do is to swing by and take about 15 minutes to explain the program to your staff. What's the best time of day to get them together for 15-20 minutes? At their lunch break? Great, I've got noon free on both Tuesday and Friday of next week. I can bring pizza and talk to everybody while they're eating. Which of those days works best for you?"

Jim's *Savage Sales Secrets* for achieving *high productivity without high pressure* are his relaxed approach, his use of names and his assumptive technique. He talks about things that he and his customer have in common like a common friendship or a common interest in golf. He makes the presentation to the employees sound easy and non-threatening. It is a no-brainer for the boss and it offers an advantage to the employees at no cost to the company.

Training sales secrets

I asked Pat Fuller how he trains his new recruits.

"Most of our training is out in the field. Our motto is *earn while you learn*. The new associate sets an appointment. The experienced manager comes in and makes the sales pitch. But he or she also teaches the new associate how to make the sale. The best part for the new person is that he earns the full commission all at once."

I was amazed. This was one of the most generous programs for new salespeople I had ever encountered in all my years in sales management and consulting with many companies. I asked Pat how the manager was motivated to do this.

"We have our own *Fireball Series* in which each District Coordinator can qualify for a bonus each quarter. Also, if the Associate gets an award, the District Coordinator gets a bonus. Everyone is motivated."

Pat went on to tell me about stock. I loved to hear about this, because one of my most important *Savage Sales Secrets* has always been to motivate salespeople with stock and to make them feel like owners.

Growth of Aflac

Aflac remains a conservative company in its investment strategy. At the end of its first year, 1955, it had $388,000 in assets. Fifty three years later, it had over $59 billion in assets with 40 million policyholder's world wide. It is listed on the New York Stock Exchange and is a Fortune 500 company.

It all starts with a visit to an office and a chat with the receptionist. I asked Pat Fuller how he does it. "I try to develop rapport with the receptionist and get the name of the decision-maker. Whenever possible, naturally, I try to have a referral."

"How does it work?"

"Hi! I'm Pat Fuller. Are you Susie? Great! I'm with Aflac. Have you heard of us? I was just checking to find out who makes decisions about insurance."

"That would probably be Arlene, our Human Resources Director."

"Great! Would you please see if Arlene has time to make an appointment with me?"

"Hi, Arlene! This is Pat Fuller with Aflac. I was just finishing up a call next door and was wondering if I could schedule a time to meet to discuss Aflac."

That often works. If not, you can almost always follow up at a later date and again ask for the appointment date.

I asked Pat if he trained his Aflac Associates to do telemarketing.

"Not much. We like to make the calls in person. The more activity an associate generates, the more appointments they will set up and the more appointments one has, the likelihood of writing business increases. That seems to work better for us. We teach them how to develop a relationship with the receptionist, often referred to as the gate-keeper. We get the receptionist to help us get to the decision maker in the business."

"What is your ideal size company?"

"I like 3-25 employees. It is easy to go to the owner of a small business. It is easier to make the sale."

"What about big corporations?"

"We do it. But we often call it '*chasing elephants*.' I have been trying to get into a big hospital for more than seven years. I have gone through two presidents of the hospital. My father-in-law was even on the board of directors. I still don't have them. But I haven't given up!"

Referrals sales secrets

Pat feels strongly that one of the main keys to his success is to continually ask for referrals. Aflac has established a "Wish List" to help broaden his client base. When he is talking with a person whom he considers a "center of influence" he will ask a question like this:

"Joe, what I'm wishing for is a CPA. I'm trying to get a CPA who may be interested in the Aflac products you have offered to your employees. Do you know any CPA's you might refer me to?"

Whether Pat has sold insurance to Joe or not, he can often get a few good names. Also he can change the category in his "Wish List" in order to stimulate the other person's imagination. "Joe, what I'm wishing for is this: I'm trying to get a surgeon. Do you know a surgeon?" Bingo! Several surgeons are now in Pat's "wish list." He can call any of them and set up an appointment to talk to their staff about Aflac.

Pat has no magic formula for success. He follows the same old patterns that successful salespeople have always used to get to the top:

- Hustle
- Elbow Grease
- Hard Work

To be more precise, Pat encourages each of his Associates to make 50 visits per week. Out of these 50 visits, each person should get 15 appointments to see a decision maker. From these 15 appointments, they should make seven presentations to employees. If they do that, they WILL be successful.

- Apply this method to your business.
- Figure out your own success formula.
- Follow it religiously.
- You *will* be successful.

---

www.aflac.com

Savage Sales Secret #28

Develop customer loyalty by thorough preparation

Herb Kristal has been my insurance professional for over 30 years. I stuck with him because I trusted him to handle everything right. He was always prepared for every meeting we ever had. He always *got high productivity without high pressure.* He was always a complete gentleman and a total professional.

He handled all my personal insurance as well as the insurance for our company. A few years ago, he suggested that we consider putting all our insurance in a trust. I consulted my attorney, Alan Lampert. Alan called Herb and talked at length about setting up the trust. After he finished, he called me and said, "Steve, I have dealt with a lot of insurance agents over the years, but Herb is the most thorough professional with whom I have ever talked."

A few years ago, Herb decided to retire and turn over his insurance clients to his associate, Steve Krochmal. At first I was concerned, because I had grown so comfortable with Herb over the years. But it did not take long for me to learn that Steve had been a great student and was just as dedicated to being a true insurance professional as was his mentor.

Recently, as I was preparing this chapter, I asked them to join me on a conference call so we could talk about their philosophy and techniques of the insurance business. I told them that their "secrets" would be of huge benefit to thousands of other insurance agents around the world. Typically, they were happy to share their thoughts. They have always been unselfish with their time and their ideas.

I began by saying, "Herb, you have sold me a lot of insurance over the years, but I never felt like you were "selling" me. Somehow, whenever I bought insurance from you, I did it calmly, with confidence, even with enthusiasm. How do you do it?"

Herb said, "Well, I try to find out what the person feels about protection for the family. I ask them how they feel about financial security. What does he want to do? What would happen if he died?

"Often I would get the client thinking by saying, 'Let's assume life insurance was never invented. Let's figure out all of the ways your family could get income if you were not here. Let's look at all the assets you have. List your income-producing assets and your non-income producing assets. Your car is an asset, but no income. Your house is an asset, but no income. Let's look at your savings, investments and any trusts you may have that will provide income for your family.'"

I jumped in and said, "Yes! Herb, that's it. You had me doing most of the talking! That's one of my *Savage Sales Secrets* and I think I may have learned it from you! I have always taught salespeople to let their clients do at least 50% of the talking. You are one of the best examples I know. Most salespeople tend to talk way too much.

Herb replied, "I always let people finish what they are saying. I never interrupt. Even if they say 'Life insurance is lousy!' I just let them get it off their chest."

Agenda sales secrets

I recalled, "Herb, it seems to me you always had an agenda for each meeting we ever had. Do you do that with every client?"

"Almost always. I have a sheet called 'Items for Discussion.' At the beginning of our meeting, I review the items on this list and say that these are some things we might cover at this meeting. The list would usually include items like:

- Assets and Liabilities – total asset picture
- Beneficiary arrangements
- Pros and cons of leaving assets in trust for your spouse, children and/or grandchildren rather than leaving money and assets to them outright.

"I actually have a list of 60-70 things and I pick out the ones that are the most meaningful to this particular client. That way I don't have to rethink it every time."

"What are some of the most common things that you would use in almost every presentation?"

"We review their total asset picture. I ask them about their current life insurance and what their family can expect to receive if they die. I ask them if they have a will or a trust. It is amazing how many people haven't done that. It gets them thinking about the future of their children and lays the groundwork for the rest of the discussion."

You can see that Herb's approach accomplishes several things:

1. It keeps the conversation organized.
2. It keeps the focus on the client, not the salesperson.
3. It engages the client and automatically gets him or her to do at least 50% of the talking.
4. It is a "visual" so the client "sees" as well as "hears" the presentation.
5. It is low-keyed, so you can *get high productivity without high pressure.*

Professional close sales secrets

"Herb," I said, "I am sure you 'closed' me many times. I am a salesperson and am always looking for sales signs, but I never felt like you were actually closing the sale. You were so soft and easy. How did you actually **close** the sale?"

"Most of the time I did not do it on the first meeting. If they agreed they needed life insurance, I would say, 'Let's have you examined and work out the details later. We can have the examiner come to your office or to your home. We'll get you cleared and see what you can get and then we can work out the details of a plan for you.'"

"Aha!" I exclaimed. You just got me to get a medical exam and I was really buying a life insurance policy!"

Herb chuckled. "Another good way to get a commitment in a very non-threatening manner is to talk about a deposit. 'Even if you haven't decided what you want to do, you might want to make a deposit. It's refundable, but if something happens to you after the exam, the insurance company **must** take you if you were OK when you took the exam.' That way you can move the process along in a way that is comfortable for the client without pressure. If they hem and haw, you need to find out the real objection."

Herb added, "Another way to make it easy for the client is to say something like this: "It takes time to make decisions and I know you want to make the right decision about this. The insurance company needs one to three months to think about it, so what you can do is sign the application and send it in to the insurance company. This will obligate the insurance company but it won't obligate you."

Steve Krochmal had been listening to his mentor. Then he added, "Herb took good care of them. Any of his clients that I have inherited have been easy to work with."

I asked, "How do you handle objections? What if they say they are not interested?"

Steve replied, "I need to ask more questions. I listen to their situation, take notes and keep relaxed. If they say they are not interested, it means I have not figured out their needs and have to do a better analysis. If I have prepared the groundwork, that objection rarely comes up. I can always refer to something they said in the conversation. For example, 'You said you wanted the family to have $100,000 per year if you died. Right now, you have only $45,000.' I simply refer to what they have already told me. Thus, it is their words, not mine."

Then the three of us talked about the emotional part of selling. Steve said, "I hate rejection!" Herb and I immediately chimed in, "I do too!" We laughed. We were all veteran salespeople and now we were admitting the truth! Herb continued, *"Every salesperson hates rejection! But we just learn to relax and not take it personally.* We learn that the person is just rejecting our product—they are not rejecting us as human beings!"

> - Yes! Take heart as you absorb the wisdom of a person who has been successful in sales for more than half a century!

First-class service with first-class stamps

Just as I was completing this chapter I got a letter from Steve Krochmal a few days before the latest postal increase. Included were several "forever" stamps. Steve reminded us that postal rates were going up in a few days and he sent us a few stamps so we wouldn't get surprised. I remembered that he had done this several times over the years, always sending us a few stamps before each postage-rate hike. It is a brilliant move, typical of Steve's little bonuses that make you love to do business with him.

Steve also sends a monthly newsletter filled with valuable financial advice. And on special occasions, like birthdays or anniversaries, he surprises us with fruit baskets or delicious chocolates. As we ended our conversation, I said, "Steve, that is one thing that both Herb and you have done so well over the years. You always provide an extra value added to your service. By doing these additional things, we keep coming back to you for all our insurance needs."

http://www.kkponline.com

Savage Sales Secret #29

Sell by finding a need and filling it

YoNaturals was founded in April, 2006 and has grown dramatically since then. Mark Trotter saw a tremendous opportunity in the schools in Southern California. Schools were under a lot of pressure to get rid of "junk food" and to provide good healthy food for the children.

A friend of Mark's had done a similar project in Australia, selling 250 vending machines full of healthy, organic food. He had proven that people would buy organic food from vending machines. Mark had experience selling photo vending machines in the USA, United Kingdom and Australia. The time was ripe to test the concept in California.

Mark spent several days at Trader Joe's and Whole Foods markets, watching what people buy. Then he selected his first line of products and set up ten vending machines in a few schools, as well as at Camp Pendleton, a Marine base near San Diego.

His approach to the schools was straightforward, the kind of honest, low-pressure approach I recommend in my *Savage Sales Secrets*. Mark would talk to a principal of a high school and say, "Hi, I'm Mark with *YoNaturals*. We are helping schools get rid of junk food and replacing it with organic food. Have you heard about us yet? OK. We are working to help school districts get rid of junk food mandated by nutrition policies. What types of vending machines do you have right now?"

The principal would usually admit, in an embarrassed tone, that his vending machines were full of sugary products that were adding to the obesity problem among America's youth.

Mark then went on to show the principal that the vending machine would not only help with the obesity problem, but would be profitable for the school as well. A school could earn $1,500 to $7,500 per machine during a typical semester.

In addition, the organic foods actually tasted great. Mark would give the principal a sample. He had juices and nutritional bars. They were just as tasty as the sugar drinks and chocolate bars that made kids fat! The principal was sold.

Mark's original goal was to sell 10 vending machines in Southern California. His original goal was reached in just a few weeks. Thus, he started thinking bigger.

It was now time to think in terms of a nationwide program. In January, 2007, he launched a major marketing program. The timing was perfect. Just two years earlier, the William J. Clinton Foundation had joined with the American Heart Association to form the Alliance for a Healthier Generation. Then in 2007, Governor Arnold Schwarzenegger of California joined the Alliance and served as a co-lead along with President Bill Clinton and the President of the American Heart Association, Tim Gardner, MD.

The goal of the Alliance is "to stop the nationwide increase in child obesity by 2010 and to take bold, innovative steps to help all children live longer and healthier lives."

Mark decided to sell distributorships, in which each distributor would service five to ten vending machines. He would guarantee each distributor, "We can get the locations for you. All you have to do is get the products and keep the machines supplied."

YoNaturals set up twelve warehouses across the country and offers free delivery. Only their customers are allowed to buy their products. They send the products directly to the schools.

In 2008, while the nation was facing a severe recession, *YoNaturals doubled its sales over 2007!*

YoNaturals has installed another innovation that has helped both schools and distributors: a wireless device from the machine that tells them what to stock.

My daughter Cynthia is now involved with *YoNaturals*. It is a perfect environment for her because she is passionate about organic foods and she is great at sales. She has used many of the principles she learned as a student salesperson selling books door-to-door during the summer. She gets *high productivity without high pressure.*

When Mark first started the business, he was able to see a lot of the potential clients face-to-face. Now, however, the company has gone nationwide. Therefore, most of Cynthia's selling is on the phone. She has two types of sales tasks:

1. To sell distributorships
2. To sell locations for the vending machines (mostly schools, but also stores, sports centers and other locations).

Selling a distributorship sales secrets

When Cynthia calls a prospective distributor, she starts out by using the *Savage Sales Strategy* of asking a lot of questions. Most salespeople tend to talk too much.

- If you ask a lot of questions, you automatically *get the customer to talk at least 50% of time,* usually more.
- Thus, Cynthia can analyze the person's needs, goals and financial objectives.
- She can also find out whether the person has enough money to invest in a distributorship.

Certain points appeal to just about every prospective distributor. "You will be on the cutting edge. You will be providing healthy food to kids in your area. You will be running your own business. You don't have to worry about getting fired because you are the boss. This is something that works great even in a down economy." (The company grew in 2008 when most companies were sinking due to the recession.)

Cynthia paints the dream, but then gets down to hard numbers. This, of course, is what a distributor needs to know if he or she is going to invest their savings in a business. "Let's say you buy five machines at $10,000 each. That's an investment of $50,000. I'm sure the big question in your mind is: How soon will you get your money back? Every time someone buys a product, we call it a "vend." Our products range from $1.00 to $2.25. The average is $1.65. You earn an average of about 65¢ on each product. Typically you will have 100 vends per day, so you will make $65 per machine per day. At that rate your ROI (return on investment) will be six months. After six months, you will be making a clear profit of $65 per machine per day. With five machines, you will be making $325 per day. With ten machines, you will earn $650 per day. All you have to do is keep them stocked. And our electronic data system will tell you exactly what products you need to refill. You generally visit each location every two or three days."

You can see how an aspiring entrepreneur would want to jump into this opportunity. Analyze the sales presentation. Remember the keys: ask a lot of questions, figure out the person's needs and objectives, paint the picture, create the dream, calculate the hard numbers and close the sale.

Selling a location

One of the great things about being a *YoNaturals* distributor is that the company helps find great locations for the vending machines. Cynthia calls schools in the distributor's area. This is what she says:

"Hi, I'm calling from *YoNaturals*. We are a healthy vending machine company. We are interested in donating a machine to your school. Who may I speak to about this?"

Sometimes Cynthia will get the principal of the school. Other times it will be the food services manager. Once she gets the decision-maker on the phone, the conversation goes something like this:

"Hi! I'm Cynthia with *YoNaturals*. Are you Joe Johnson, the principal?"

"Yes."

"Great! We have a few healthy organic vending machines and we would like to give one to your school. You will get a share of the profit. And we do all the work. We maintain, monitor and stock our machines."

Cynthia says that the key is to be friendly and relaxed. "You don't want them to feel they are being used. They believe me and trust me. They feel like I'm a friend."

I asked her if she talked about the huge problem of obesity in America. "I don't make a big deal out of it. I talk about my own kids and what I feed them. We chat about the shifting paradigms of what is considered healthy. I have lots of experience with health food. They always are impressed when I mention that our foods have no preservatives, no dyes and no transfats."

YoNaturals is a great example of how you can take an issue that is currently "hot" in the market and make an exciting business out of it. You can sell in person or over the phone. No matter which method you choose, you need to remember to do the opposite of what most sales people do: *don't talk too much*!

- Make sure the *customer does at least 50% of the talking,* whether on the phone or in person.
- Do this, and you will *get high productivity without high pressure.*

---

http://www.yonaturals.com

Savage Sales Secrets Summarized

How you can build robust sales systems that will take you to new levels of profitability

In this book you have learned many secrets that will transform your ability to be a great sales manager and leader. The highlights that apply to you, no matter what you are selling, are these:

- You can get high production without high pressure.
- You can control the conversation more by talking less—and letting the customer talk.
- You should ask a lot of questions and avoid the temptation to talk too much.
- You can discover your customer's needs by listening instead of talking.
- You can increase your company's market share and the loyalty of your customers by making your company easy to do business with.
- You can turn your sales force into your most productive asset by giving them power to make decisions and a chance to share in the company's equity.
- You can <u>stop</u> your customers from grinding you down on price and you can turn those same customers into evangelists for your company by giving them incredible service.
- You can get your sales, operations and administrative people all playing on the same team by getting all your managers out in the trenches.

- You can make it more <u>fun</u> for people to work together by making your company a place of positive energy and joy.
- You can turn ordinary salespeople into motivated superstars by treating them like heroes.
- You can make your customers so happy they wouldn't <u>dream </u>of doing business with anyone else by giving them more than they expected.
- You can make the tough decisions, so you have confidence when you decide what you need to keep, and what you need to let go of, but still let your subordinates make most of the decisions.
- You can identify new markets, and profitably expand into those markets while avoiding the pitfalls—especially in foreign markets.
- You, the business leader, can use your personal qualities so your people <u>want</u> to carry out your vision.
- You can get everyone in your organization excited about—and committed to—making your business more profitable!

A quick start to Savage Sales Secrets

In this book you have learned dozens of ways you can apply *Savage Sales Secrets* to build your business. But to make it easy, just start with three, right now. Go back to work tomorrow and start with three simple steps. Apply these *Savage Sales Secrets* immediately.

> 1. Drive one decision down.
> 2. Go on one sales call.
> 3. Eliminate one rule.
>
> Have the courage to change.

<u>www.stevesavage.com</u>

GET YOUR FREE GIFT!
As Promised On The Front Cover…

Get a Free Subscription to
Savage Strategies

Learn practical and powerful ideas that are guaranteed
to transform your business. These are practical and
powerful tips from a genuine "Savage guerrilla"
who has spent his lifetime in the trenches.

Get all back issues – free – plus all future issues.

Each newsletter is one page long, so you can get everything
you need fast. You will get great tips on marketing,
sales and business building. You will also hear about
Steve's experiences working with companies around
the world and how they apply to your business.

You will learn how to:

- Get High Productivity without High Pressure
- Drive Decisions Downward
- Get in the Trenches
- Make it Easy for your Customers
- Elevate your Salespeople
- Eliminate Rules
- Make Everyone Feel Important
- Avoid "Voice Jail"
- Sell More by Talking Less
- Close More with Soft Sales Techniques
- And Much More!

> **To get Savage Strategies Free Right Now:**
> **www.stevesavage.com/killertransformations**
> **Then subscribe to Savage Strategies.**

About Steve Savage

Steve Savage is an acclaimed sales and management strategist who has helped dozens of companies dramatically increase their sales and profits.

Steve's strategies are based on a lifetime of building companies throughout the Western Hemisphere. He has achieved many dazzling successes (and a few failures). He took one company from zero to $60 million in six years and sold it to Colgate Palmolive.

His academic credentials are solid, with a BA in philosophy from Wheaton College and an MBA in marketing from Michigan State University (magna cum laude). However, his marketing and sales tactics do not come from the ivory tower. They come straight from the trenches.

Jay Levinson, author of *Guerrilla Marketing* (20 million copies sold) describes Steve Savage as "the most brilliant and gutsy guerrilla marketer I have ever known."

Steve is the co-author with Jay Levinson of *Guerrilla Business Secrets*, *58 Ways to Start, Build and Sell Your Business.*

Steve is a powerful public speaker. He has worked with corporate CEO's in promoting culture change to make each company totally customer oriented. His topics include:

- Get High Productivity without High Pressure
- Guerrilla Marketing
- Corporate Culture Change
- Create a Sales Empire
- Help Everyone in the Company Think like a Salesperson – Even the Accountants!
- Doing Business in Mexico and Latin America
- Increasing Your Sales in the Hispanic Community
- Drive Decisions Downward
- Eliminate Rules
- Give Power to Your Salespeople
- Make Your Company Easy

Steve grew up in Ecuador, the son of missionary parents. He is 100% bilingual and gives seminars in both English and Spanish. He has built eighteen companies in eight countries. He has influenced the lives of thousands of people throughout the world, elevating their self confidence, teaching them sound business techniques and showing them how to be genuine *Savage Sales Champions*.

BUY A SHARE OF THE FUTURE IN YOUR COMMUNITY

These certificates make great holiday, graduation and birthday gifts that can be personalized with the recipient's name. The cost of one S.H.A.R.E. or one square foot is $54.17. The personalized certificate is suitable for framing and will state the number of shares purchased and the amount of each share, as well as the recipient's name. The home that you participate in "building" will last for many years and will continue to grow in value.

Here is a sample SHARE certificate:

THIS CERTIFIES THAT
YOUR NAME HERE
HAS INVESTED IN A HOME FOR A DESERVING FAMILY
1985-2005
TWENTY YEARS OF BUILDING FUTURES IN OUR
COMMUNITY ONE HOME AT A TIME
1200 SQUARE FOOT HOUSE @ $65,000 = $54.17 PER SQUARE FOOT
This certificate represents a tax deductible donation. It has no cash value.

YES, I WOULD LIKE TO HELP!

I support the work that Habitat for Humanity does and I want to be part of the excitement! As a donor, I will receive periodic updates on your construction activities but, more importantly, I know my gift will help a family in our community realize the dream of homeownership. **I would like to SHARE in your efforts against substandard housing in my community!** *(Please print below)*

PLEASE SEND ME _____ SHARES at $54.17 EACH = $ $_____

In Honor Of: _____

Occasion: (Circle One)   HOLIDAY   BIRTHDAY   ANNIVERSARY

         OTHER: _____

Address of Recipient: _____

Gift From: _____ *Donor Address:* _____

Donor Email: _____

I AM ENCLOSING A CHECK FOR $ $_____ PAYABLE TO HABITAT FOR HUMANITY OR PLEASE CHARGE MY VISA OR MASTERCARD *(CIRCLE ONE)*

Card Number _____ Expiration Date: _____

Name as it appears on Credit Card _____ Charge Amount $ _____

Signature _____

Billing Address _____

Telephone # Day _____ Eve _____

PLEASE NOTE: Your contribution is tax-deductible to the fullest extent allowed by law.
Habitat for Humanity • P.O. Box 1443 • Newport News, VA 23601 • 757-596-5553
www.HelpHabitatforHumanity.org